Complete Ninja Foodi Cookbook UK 2021

:

Quick & Easy Tender crispy Ninja Foodi Recipes to Prepare Delicious Meals Using Metric Measurement

Charlie Goodwin

ISBN-13 : 979-8500562906

This document is geared towards providing exact and reliable information in regards to the topic and issue covered. The publication is sold with the idea that the publisher is not required to render accounting, officially permitted, or otherwise, qualified services. If advice is necessary, legal or professional, a practiced individual in the profession should be ordered.

Table Of Contents

Introduction

What exactly is the Ninja Foodi?

At its heart, the Ninja Foodi is an electric pressure cooker, but behind its seemingly innocent façade, it's much more than that. Well, Ninja Foodi is perhaps the latest and one of the most skillful and modern multi-cooker to date that every chef and budding enthusiast should have!

It's not only blends all the qualities of a contemporary electric pressure cooker such as an Instant Pot but also adds the extra benefit of being capable to Air Fryer using the same device! And does so by utilizing it's patented "Tender Crisp" technology, which we will talk about soon. Thus this is the finest kitchen gadget as a cooking appliance.

But asides from the built-in details of being an electric pressure cooker and an Air Fryer, the Ninja Foodi also can used as a steamer, slow cooker, browning pan, air crisper, roaster, broiler, and even a dehydrator!

This mostly means that using the Ninja Foodi, you will achieve the power to make your favorite Keto-Friendly dish ranging from stews, meat, snacks, and even desserts!

Using the dehydrator feature, the Ninja Foodi will also allow you to preserve and fruits and vegetables.

And for the best part? Despite having a myriad of fascinating features, the Ninja is still a very handy and user-friendly machine that everyone can use!

Understanding the "TenderCrisp Technology"

The TenderCrisp Technology is probably the foundation feature that makes the Ninja Foodi so unique and appealing to.

Before moving on to the other features, it is essential that you have a good understanding of what this technology literally means and how it will affect your cooking style if you prefer using the Foodi.

So, consider this.

Whenever you will use a pressure cooker to cook hardy ingredients related to poultry meat or any other rough meat, you normally get food that is very juicy and wonderful to eat. However, you easily the act of pressure cooking won't be effective to produce meat that is both tenders on the inside and crispy on the outside.

And so the appliances such as "Air Fryers" created so that an individual can produce deliciously tender and juicy meals, with a pleasant crispy finish.

The Ninja Foodi incorporates this amazing cooking style of Air Fryers and inspires the art of Pressure Cooking and Air Frying into one complete package.

So substantially, using the Ninja Foodi, at first you will be able to pressure cook your meat to a very juicy and tender finish, and end it with a nice crispy exterior.

The crispiness is achieved in the Ninja Foodi using the installed Crisping Lid alongside the Crisping Basket, combined with the appliance.

A technique known as the "AirCrisp" mode starts the crisping action.

This complete process of first pressure cooking and then crisping the meals in a single pot using their crisping basket and Air Crisper is known as their patented "TenderCrisp" technology.

Including this amazing tech immediately makes this appliance one of a kind and ultimately separates itself from the rest of the crowd.

What to expect inside the box

Assuming that you are going to buy a new Ninja Foodi or have purchased one but haven't open it yet, below is a summary of what you might expect when you open up a box for the first time.

The Pressure Lid

The Crisping Lid

A 1,400 Watt Housing Unit

A 6 and ½ quart ceramic coated pot

A Stainless-Steel reversible Steam/Broil rack

4-quart Ceramic Coated Cook/Crisping Basket

Cook and Crisp Layered Insert

An included recipe book that covers 45 recipes

However, if you want to completely unleash the full potential of the appliance, you should consider purchasing these additional components as they will help you in the long run. Keep in mind that none of these are included in the pot itself and if you want them, you have to purchase them separately.

Multi-Purpose Pan

Crisper Pan

Loaf Pan

Dehydrating Pan

Roasting Pan Inse

Understanding the basics of the control panel

If you want to quickly master the art of using your Ninja Foodi, the first thing that you should know about is how the various buttons on the control panel work. Each button has its own purpose and having a good understanding of all them will allow you to create amazing recipes in no time!

At first, let me talk about the core buttons, after which I will discuss a little bit about the various functions.

Standby

This is self-explanatory, if the Ninja Foodi stays idle for 10 minutes, it will automatically go into Standby mode until further command.

Power

This button allows you to turn your appliance on or off.

Keep Warm

This button allows you Ninja Foodi to keep the food at a food-safe temperature for a prolonged period of time.

Start/Stop

Once the cooking temperature has been set, you can use the start/stop button to stop or initiate the cooking process.

Time Arrow

The time arrows allow you to set the timer for your cooking mode.

Temp Arrow

The temp arrow allows you to set the temperature for your appliance.

Preset Cooking

The Pre-Set cooking button allows you to choose one of the 8 built-in cooking modes and choose the best one suitable for your meal. The different functions are broken down in the next section

The Core Functionalities of the Foodi

With the TenderCrisp tech out of the way, let me talk a little bit about the different buttons and features found in the Foodi.

The following guide should help you understand what each of the buttons does and how you can use them to their fullest extent.

Pressure

The Pressure Button will allow you to simply Pressure Cook your foods using the Ninja Foodi. This will allow you to cook meals almost 70% faster than other traditional methods. Keep in mind that if you use the Pressure Button, you will also get the option to release the pressure naturally or perform a quick release pressure in the end.

Releasing the pressure naturally is often recommended for tough meats while the quick release is often suited for tender cuts like fish or even vegetables.

Steam

This particular button allows you to use the "Steam" function of the Ninja Foodi. Using steam, you will be able to cook very delicate food at high temperatures. Just make sure to use at least a cup of liquid when steaming your food. While using this feature, make sure to use the Pressure Lid.

Slow Cooker

This particular button will allow you to utilize the Slow Cooker mode that allows you to use the Ninja Foodi as a traditional Slow Cooker. Through this method, your cooks will be cooked at a very low temperature over a prolonged period of time. The time can be adjusted from 12-4 hours, and once the cooking is done, the appliance will automatically switch to "KEEP WARM" function where the meal stays hot until you open it up.

Sear/Saute

This particular button allows you to use your Ninja Foodi to brown meat. This feature is excellent when you need searing or browning meat/ Sautéing spices. This same function can also be used to simmer sauces. Similar to Broil mode, this does not come with a temperature setting, rather, once you are done browning, you simply need to press the "START/STOP" button to initiate or stop the process.

Air Crisp

This is possibly the most unique feature of the Ninja Foodi. Using the Air Crisp feature, you will be able to use your Ninja Foodi as an Air Fryer, that allows you to add a nice crispy and crunchy texture with little to almost no oil. This particular setting cooks the food at extremely high temperatures of 149 °C to 204°C. As a general tip, it is advised that you pre-heat the appliance before adding your ingredients for best results. Needless to say, this feature uses the Crisping lid.

Bake/Roast

This particular function is for those who like to bake! The Bake/Roast function is an awesome mode that allows users to seamlessly use their Foodi as a regular oven (thanks to crisping lid) that allows them to create inspiring baked goods.

Broil

The Broil feature is used in conjunction with the Crisping Lid in order to slightly brown or caramelizes the surface of your food. It cooks food at a higher temperature to create the required brown surface. Keep in mind that this feature has no temperature adjustment.

Dehydrate

The Dehydrate function allows you to dehydrate food between 41 °C and 91 °C, and this feature will allow you to make healthy dried snacks out of meat, vegetables, and fruits. However, if you want to use this device, it is advised that you purchase a dehydrating rack for maximum efficiency

Looking at the different Core parts of the Ninja Foodi

Now that you are familiar with the basics of the Ninja Foodi, let me walk you through the core parts of your Ninja Foodi to help you to further familiarize yourself with the appliance itself.

In short, there are 5 core components of your Ninja Foodi that you should know about.

Pressure Lid

The pressure lid turns your Ninja Foodi into a fine electric pressure that allows you to cook your food efficiently and quickly using the power of pressure.

Crisping Lid

The Crisping lid adapts the fan and temperature of the Ninja Foodi so that you use the Air Crisp feature, alongside bake/Roast, broil and dehydrate mode.

The powerful fan present rotates at 2500 rpm and distributes heat all around your meal. Temperatures up to 233 °C can be reached using this method. On the other side of the spectrum, you can set the temperature to as low as 38 °C as well, this allows you to dehydrate vegetables, fruits, meats etc.

Cooking Pot

The Ninja Foodie's cooking pot is carefully designed with the extra-wide diameter to ensure that you are able to use to not only pressure cook your meals, but Saute and sear vegetables and meat when needed. The Nano ceramic coating of the pot ensures that you can cook anything you want! However, always make sure to use wooden or silicone utensils with the appliance.

Cook and Crisp Basket

This particular basket is specifically designed to ensure that you are able to efficiently Air Crisp your goodies when needed and get the perfect brown and crispy finish.

Reversible Rack

In the lower position, the provided Reversible Rack will actually allow you to steam vegetables and fish rapidly. On the other hand, if you flip the rack and in a higher position, you can use it broil goodies and give them a nice crispy finish.

Now that the basics of the Ninja Foodi are covered, let me share some other information that should be helpful to you

Why is the Ninja Foodi so amazing?

Wholesome 360 Meals

The Ninja Foodi actually allows you to make a wide variety of healthy meals with various different components using just a single pot. You can quickly cook your desired meat on the bottom while adding veggies on top using the reversible rack. Each individual part of your meal will get an even and fine texture in the end that will provide a fine and satisfying meal.

One Pot that does it all

I cannot stress this enough, the versatility of the Ninja Foodi is what makes them so unique. Using the TenderCrisp tech, you will be able to turn simple recipes like soups and stews into amazing Wonders! Alternatively, using the pressure cooking feature, you will simply cook stews, chilis, casseroles, and even desserts! The list goes on. As a matter of fact, the crisping lid also allows you to bake biscuits too!

Defrost-Be Gone

The Ninja Foodi is one of that rare appliance that actually allows you to directly cook frozen meals, saving a lot of time. The pressure method can easily defrost and tenderize frozen meat, while the Crisping Lid will allow you to get a fine crispy finish.

Restaurant Quality Dish At Home

Yes, you read that right! Using the Ninja Foodi and its patented Air Crisping technology, you can even create restaurant style BBQ meals in an instant! A fine 5-pound chicken, beef brisket, pork belly! Nothing is off limits when you have the power of the Ninja Foodi with you.

Saves space in Kitchen

The versatility of the Ninja Foodi and its capacity act as multiple appliances allow you to get rid of the steamer, Saute pan, slow cooker, pressure cooker and a myriad of different appliances and use the Ninja Foodi for everything.

High-Pressure kills microbes

The excellent way in which the Ninja Foodi cook, ensure that the temperature inside is able to reach sufficiently high enough levels during pressure cooking to ensure that 99% of harmful microbes are killed during the process. In fact, the Ninja Foodi is even able to kill significantly more resistant microbes as well.

Amazing tips for the perfect "TenderCrisp"

Using the TenderCrisp technology to create appealing crispy meals might seem a little bit intimated at first. The following tips should help you during your early days and make things easier:

¬ Always make sure to pre-heat your Ninja Foodi before using the Sear/Saute, Air Crips or Broil functions. A general method would be to pre-heat your Foodi for at least 5 minutes before adding food.

¬ It is highly recommended that you sometimes shake up your ingredients when trying to Air Fry using the Ninja Foodi. This allows for even cooking on all side. The general idea is to shake it once or twice during the whole crisping session.

¬ If you are crisping large quantity or veggies, try to drizzle a little bit of oil on top/or use a brush to cover a bit of oil on top to ensure that it is well coated.

¬ We highly advised that you try to keep the ingredients at the same size when crisping. This will allow for even cooking as well.

¬ While using rice as a general rule, it is advised that you rinse your rice thoroughly under water before adding them to the Foodi.

¬ If you are making an all-in-one-pot meal, then you may add a layer of meat to the base of the pot, place your reversible rack and place veggies/or whatever you require on the rack. This will not only help to build more flavor but will make it more convenient for you to crisp all the ingredients in one go.

Awesome general tips about the appliance

While in previous paragraph covered tips clearly given to improve your Tender Crisping experience, the following should help you in general while using Ninja foodi.

¬ Always make sure to remember that the provided "Timer" button is not necessarily included to only work as a time setting button. This button can also be used as a "Delay Timer'. Meaning, you will be able to set a specific time after which the appliance will automatically start up and cook the food.

¬ When using "Unfrozen" meat, always try to ensure that you are using the same amount of water as you would've used when cooking with frozen meat.

¬   If you find yourself in a rush, you may skip the natural pressure release system and opt for a quick release. For this, all you have to do is just naturally move the pressure valve to "Open" position. However, you have to keep in mind that release the pressure in such a way might be a little uncertain as a lot of pressure gets released at once. So be watchful

¬   You should know that the proper isolation of the lid is essential to productive cooking in the Ninja Foodi. So, always double check and be assured that the silicon ring is placed strongly all around the groove of the Ninja Foodi.

¬   Before pressure cooking, make it certain that your pressure valve is set in the position labeled "Locked", otherwise your Ninja Foodi won't be able to build up the pressure.

¬   If you are entirely new to utilizing a Ninja Foodi, you may find yourself a little bit puzzled by the term "Release pressure naturally". Well, all you have to do to release pressure normally is simply let your device launch pressure by itself after the timer reaches "0". It would certainly take about 10-15 mins for the pressure to find down to safe levels.

Chapter 1-Breakfast Recipes

Sausage Cheese Frittata

Prep Time: 15 min
Cooking time: 20 min
Servings: 2
Ingredients:
- **1/4 lb./114gm** breakfast sausage, heated and smashed
- 1 red bell pepper, chopped
- 4 eggs, trampled
- **1/2 cup/ 42 g** cheddar cheese, ragged
- 1 green onion, sliced
- Cooking spray

Directions:
1. Spray a small baking pan with oil.
2. Blend the eggs, sausage, cheese, onion and bell pepper.
3. Transfer the egg mix into the pan.
4. Cook at 360°F/ °C/183°C for almost 20 min In "Air Crisp" cooking mode.
5. Serve warm.

Butter Dipped Broccoli Florets

Prep Time: 10 min
Cooking time: 8 min
Servings: 4
Ingredients:
- 4 tbsp/ 56.7 g butter
- 2 pounds/ 907g broccoli buds
- Salt and black pepper, for taste
- 1 cup/120g whip cream

Directions:
1. Place a carrier in the bottom of your Ninja Foodi and add water
2. Put broccoli buds on top of the carrier.
3. Lock the Ninja Foodi's lid and cook on "Pressure" mode at High for 5 min
4. Quick-release pressure and move florets to the pot
5. Season with salt, pepper and add butter
6. Lock the Crisping Lid and Air Crisp on 360°F/ °C/183°C 3 min
7. Transfer to a serving plate.

Egg Turkey Cups

Prep Time: 10 min
Cooking time: 10 min
Servings: 4
Ingredients:

- 8 tbsp/64g turkey sausage, cooked and smashed, separated
- 8 tbsp/15 **g** frozen spinach, sliced and separated
- 8 tsp/40g sliced in grater cheddar cheese, divided
- 4 eggs

Directions:

1. Add a layer of the sausage, spinach and cheese on each muffin cup.
2. Crack the egg open on top. Seal the crisping lid. Select "Air Crisp" cooking mode.
3. Cook at 330 °F/ °C / 166°C for almost 10 min.

Roasted Potatoes

Prep Time: 30 min
Cooking time: 20 min
Servings: 6
Ingredients:

- 2 tsp/6.56 **g** garlic powder
- 2 tbsp/27 ml olive oil
- 2 lb/910 **g** baby potatoes, cut into wedges

Directions:

1. Toss the potatoes in olive oil and garlic salt.
2. Put the potatoes to the Ninja Foodi Air Fryer's insert.
3. Cook at 390 °F/ °C / 199 °C for almost 20 min at "Air Crisp" cooking mode.

Broccoli Quiche

Prep Time: 20 min
Cooking time: 22 min
Servings: 2
Ingredients:

- 1 cup/ 237 ml of water
- 2 cups / 142 **g** broccoli buds
- 1 carrot, chopped
- 1 cup/ 235 **g** cheddar cheese, sliced in grater
- 1/4 / 150 **g** cup Feta cheese, crumbled
- 1/4 / 59 ml cup milk
- 2 eggs
- 1 teaspoon / 0.54 **g** parsley
- 1 tsp/ 0.91 **g** thyme
- Salt and black pepper, to taste

Directions:

1. Pour water and place the basket inside the Ninja Foodi.
2. Put the carrots and broccoli into the basket
3. Cook at high pressure for 2 min in "Pressure" cooking mode.
4. Release the pressure quickly.
5. Crack all the eggs in a proper bowl and beat.

6.   Add salt, pepper, parsley and thyme for seasoning
7.   Put the vegetables on a small baking pan.
8.   Layer with the cheese and pour in the beaten eggs Place in the Ninja Foodi.
9.   Cook at 350 °F/ °C / 177 °C for almost 20 min at "Air Crisp" cooking mode.
10.   Serve and Enjoy

Egg Burrito

Prep Time: 10 min
Cooking time: 10 min
Servings: 8
Ingredients:
- 3 eggs, beaten
- 2 red bell peppers, julienned
- Salt and black pepper, for taste
- 8 tortillas
- Cooking spray
- 1 onion, sliced

Directions:
1.   Scramble the eggs
2.   Add salt and black pepper. Set aside.
3.   Select sauté mode on the Ninja Foodi. Spray with the oil.
4.   Cook the vegetables until soft.
5.   Remove and set aside.
6.   Pour the eggs into the pot. Cook until firm.
7.   Wrap the eggs and veggies with a tortilla.
8.   Serve warm.

Bacon Egg Scramble

Prep Time: 10 min
Cooking time: 5 min
Servings: 2
Ingredients:
- 1 tablespoon milk
- 2 eggs
- 4 strips bacon
- Salt and black pepper, to taste

Directions:
1.   Place the bacon inside the Ninja Foodi.
2.   Cook at 390 °F/ °C / 199 °C for almost 3 min at "Air Crisp" cooking mode.
3.   Flip and cook for another 2 min. Set it aside.
4.   Whisk the eggs and milk in a bowl.
5.   Add salt and black pepper for seasoning,
6.   Put the eggs into Ninja Foodi and cook in sauté mode until firm.
7.   Serve warm.

Mushroom Omelets

Prep Time: 15 min
Cooking time: 8 min
Servings: 2
Ingredients:
- 2 eggs
- 59 ml milk
- 9.3g red bell pepper, sliced
- 1 slice ham, diced
- 7.81 g mushrooms, sliced
- Salt to taste
- 56.2 g cheese, shredded

Directions:
1. Whisk the eggs and milk and add the ham and vegetables.
2. Add the salt for seasoning.
3. Pour the mixture into a small pan.
4. Place the pan inside the Ninja Foodi Air Fryer's insert.
5. Cook at 350 °F/ °C /177 °C for almost 8 min at "Air Crisp" cooking mode.
6. On 7th Minute, sprinkle the cheese on top.
7. Serve warm.

Paprika Shrimp

Prep Time: 10 min
Cooking time: 15 min
Servings: 4
Ingredients:
- 453 g shrimps, peeled and deveined
- 28 g butter
- 1 red Chilli pepper, seeded and chopped
- 1 g smoked paprika
- Lemongrass stalks

Directions:
1. Except lemongrass mix all of the ingredients well, and marinate for 1 hour
Transfer to Ninja Foodi and cook on "Bake/Roast" cooking mode for 15 min at 174 °C
2. Serve and enjoy!

Egg Scramble

Prep Time: 10 min
Cooking time: 5-10 min
Servings: 2
Ingredients:
- 2 whole eggs
- 15 ml milk
- 4 strips bacon
- Salt and black pepper, for taste

Directions:

1. Put bacon inside your Ninja Foodi.
2. Cook for 3 min at 199 °C at "Air Crisp" cooking mode.
3. Flip and cook for 2 min more
4. Take away bacon and keep it on the side.
5. Whisk eggs and milk in a suitable bowl Season with salt and black pepper.
6. Set your Ninja Foodi to Sauté mode.
7. Add eggs, cook until firm.
8. Serve and enjoy!

Crispy Broccoli Florets

Prep Time: 10 min
Cooking time: 5 min
Servings: 4
Ingredients:
* 57 **g** butter melted
* Salt and black pepper, to taste
* 908 **g** broccoli florets
* 240 ml whipping cream
Directions:
1. Place a steamer basket and add water in your Ninja Foodi's insert
2. Place florets on top of the basket
3. Cook on "Pressure" mode at High for 5 min. Quick-release pressure
4. Transfer florets from the steamer basket to the pot. Add salt, pepper, butter, and stir
5. Lock the Crisping Lid and cook on "Air Crisp" cooking mode for 360°F/ °C/183°C.
6. Serve and enjoy!

Carrot Meal

Prep Time: 10 min
Cooking time: 4 min
Servings: 4
Ingredients:

* 680 **g** carrots, chopped
* 17.07 **g** of butter at room temperature
* 21.9 **g** of agave nectar
* 1.15 **g** of sea salt
* 237 ml of water

Directions:
1. Clean and peel your carrots properly and chop them into small pieces
2. Pour 237 ml water into Ninja Foodi's cooking pot.
3. Place the carrots in a steamer basket and put the basket inside the Ninja Foodi
4. Cook on "Pressure" mode at High for 4 min. when done quick release to remove the steam.
5. Transfer the carrots to a deep bowl and use an immersion blender to blend the carrots
6. Add butter, nectar, salt, and puree. Taste the puree and season more if needed.
7. Serve and enjoy!

Avocado Stuffed Eggs

Prep Time: 10 min
Cooking time: 5 min
Servings: 6
Ingredients:
- 7.39 ml fresh lemon juice
- 1 medium ripe avocado, peeled, pitted and chopped
- 6 eggs, boiled, peeled and cut in half lengthwise
- Salt to taste
- 34 **g** fresh watercress, trimmed

Directions:
1. Place a steamer basket at the bottom of your Ninja Foodi. Add water
2. Add watercress on the basket and Lock the Ninja Foodi's lid.
3. Cook on "Pressure" mode at High for almost 3 min, then quick release the pressure and drain the watercress
4. Remove egg yolks and transfer them to a bowl
5. Add watercress, avocado, lemon juice, salt into the bowl and mash with a fork
6. Place egg whites in a serving bowl and fill them with the watercress and avocado dish.
7. Serve and enjoy!

Avocado Egg Cups

Prep Time: 30 min
Cooking time: 15 min
Servings: 2
Ingredients:
- 1 avocado, sliced in half and pitted
- 2 eggs
- Salt and black pepper, to taste
- 58.7 **g** cheddar cheese, shredded

Directions:
1. Crack the egg and whisk
2. Pour the egg into the avocado slice.
3. For seasoning, add salt and black pepper.
4. Put it on the Ninja Foodi Air Fryer's insert.
5. Select "Air Crisp" cooking mode. Cook at 204 °C for almost 15 min.
6. Sprinkle with the cheese on 12th min before it is cooked.
7. Serve warm.

Crispy Egg Toast

Prep Time: 15 min
Cooking time: 9 min
Servings: 1
Ingredients:
- 1 slice bread
- 1 egg

- Salt and black pepper, to taste
- Cooking spray

Directions:
1. Spray a small baking pan with cooking oil.
2. Make a medium-sized hole in the center of the bread slice.
3. Crack open the egg and put it inside the hole.
4. Place the bread inside the pan.
5. Cover the Ninja Foodi with the crisping lid. Select "Air Crisp" cooking mode.
6. Cook at 330 °F/ °C /166 °C for almost 6 min.
7. Flip the toast and cook for 3 more min.
8. Serve warm.

Herbed Eggs

Prep Time: 10 min
Cooking time: 5 min
Servings: 1
Ingredients:
- Cooking spray
- 1 egg
- 5.69 g dried rosemary
- Salt and black pepper, to taste

Directions:
1. Spray a ramekin with oil. Crack the egg into the ramekin.
2. Add rosemary, salt and black pepper for seasoning
3. Close the crisping lid. Select "Air Crisp" cooking mode.
4. Cook at 330 °F/ °C / 166 °C for almost 5 min.
5. Serve warm.

Cheesy Herb Frittata

Prep Time: 15 min
Cooking time: 15 min
Servings: 4
Ingredients:
- 4 eggs
- 242 g half and half
- 28.3 g parsley, chopped
- 28.3 g chives, chopped
- 57 g shredded cheddar cheese
- Salt and black pepper, to taste

Directions:
1. Beat the eggs in a bowl. Add the rest of the ingredients and stir well.
2. Pour the mixture into a small baking pan.
3. Place the pan on top of the Ninja Foodi Air Fryer's insert.
4. Seal the crisping lid. Select "Air Crisp" cooking mode.
5. Cook at 330 °F/ °C /166 °C for almost 15 min.
6. Serve warm.

Zested Lamb Chops

Prep Time: 5 min
Cooking time: 40 min
Servings: 4

Ingredients:

- 56.7 g butter
- 48 ml lemon juice
- 4 lamb chops, with bone
- 15 g flour
- 259 g Picante sauce

Directions:

1. Coat chops with flour and keep them on the side
2. Set your Ninja Foodi to Sauté mode and add chopped butter
3. Cook in Sauté for 2 min, add Picante sauce and lemon juice
4. Tightly lock the Ninja Foodi's lid and cook on "Pressure" mode at High for 40 min.
5. Release the pressure naturally and serve.

Butter Salmon

Cooking time: 30 min   Prep Time: 10 min Servings: 6

Ingredients:

- 454 g salmon fillets
- 10.54 g ginger/garlic paste
- 3 green chilies, chopped
- Salt and black pepper, to taste
- 178 ml butter

Directions:

1. Season salmon fillets with ginger, garlic paste, salt, pepper
2. Place salmon fillets to Ninja Foodi and top with green chilies and butter
3. Lock the Ninja Foodi's lid and cook on the "Bake/Roast" cooking mode for 30 min at 360°F/ °C/183°C
4. Enjoy!

Hash Brown Casserole

Cooking time: 20 min Prep Time: 10 min Servings: 4

Ingredients:

- Cooking spray
- 1 green bell pepper, diced
- 454 g hash browns
- 1 red bell pepper, diced
- 454 g breakfast sausage, cooked and crumbled
- 1 onion, diced
- 4 eggs
- Salt and black pepper, to taste

Directions:

1. Take a small baking pan and coat it with with oil.
2. Now put the hash browns on the bottom part of the pan.
3. Add the sausage on the hash browns and then the onion and bell peppers.

4.   Now place the pan on top of the basket and Put the basket inside the Ninja   Foodi.
5.   Close the crisping lid.
6.   Cook at 350 °F/ °C / 177 °C for almost 10 min at "Air Crisp" cooking mode.
7.   Now open the lid. Crack the eggs on top.
8.   Cook for another 10 min on Saute mode.
9.   Add salt and black pepper for seasoning,.
10.   Serve warm.

Fried Eggs

Servings: 2 Cooking time: 10 min Prep Time: 5 min
Ingredients:
- 5 ml butter, melted
- 4 eggs
- 3.7 g salt
- 1.42 g teaspoon black pepper

Directions:
1.   Brush a small egg pan with butter
2.   Take an egg beater and beat the eggs in the pan very well for 2 min
3.   Sprinkle the eggs with the black pepper and salt.
4.   Take the Ninja Foodi's pot and put the pan into it.
5.   Cover the lid. Cook the egg for 10 min at 350 °F/ °C/177 °C
6.   Serve immediately and enjoy!

Nutrition Values Per Serving:
Calories: 143, Total fat: 10.2g, Carbohydrates: 0.9g, Protein: 11.4g

Tofu with Mushrooms

Servings: 2 /Cooking time: 10 min /Prep Time: 10 min
Ingredients:

- butter 113.4 g
- cubed tofu 2 blocks
- shredded parmesan cheese 117 g
- Salt and black pepper, to taste
- Chopped fresh mushrooms 250 g

Directions:
1.   mix in tofu, salt, and pepper very well in a suitable bowl.
2.   Put seasoned tofu in your ninja foodi and set it to sauté mode
3.   Sauté for 5 min
4.   Add cheese, mushroom and Sauté for 3 min.
5.   Cook on the "Air Crisp" mode for 3 min at 350 °F/ °C/177 °C .
6.   Immediately transfer to a serving plate and enjoy warm !

Nutrition Values Per Serving:
Calories: 211, Total fat: 18g, Carbohydrates: 2g, Protein: 11g

Mushroom Stir Fry

Servings: 8 Prep Time: 10 min Cooking time: 15 min
Ingredients:
- White mushrooms stems trimmed 454 g
- Unsalted butter 28.3 g
- Salt 3 **g**
- Water 59 ml

Directions:
1. Place the mushrooms, butter, and salt in your Ninja Foodi pot
2. Add water and lock the pressure lid of the ninja foodi, don't forget to seal the valve
3. Now Cook the mushrooms on "Pressure" mode at High for 5 min,
4. Quick release pressure once cooked.
5. Set your pot to HIGH Sauté mode and bring the mix to a boil over 5 min until all the water evaporates
6. Once the liquid has evaporated, stir for 1 minute until slightly browned.
7. It's time to Enjoy the meal!

Nutrition Values Per Serving:
Calories: 50, Total fat: 4g, Carbohydrates: 2g, Protein: 2g

Soupy Lamb Roast

Prep Time: 10 min Cooking time: 60 min Servings: 6
Ingredients:
- Beef broth 241 g
- Lamb roast 907 **g**
- Onion soup 237 ml
- Salt and black pepper, to taste

Directions:
1. Place the lamb roast into your Ninja Foodi pot.
2. Add the onion soup, beef broth, salt, and pepper on top of the lamb roast.
3. Cook on Medium-HIGH pressure for 55 min.
4. Naturally Release the pressure for over 10 min.
5. Serve warm!

Nutrition Values Per Serving:
Calories: 349, Total fat: 18g, Carbohydrates: 2.9g, Protein: 39g

Morning Sausage Meal

Servings: 6 Prep Time: 10 min Cooking time: 20 min
Ingredients:

- Butter 28.3 **g**
- Whole eggs 4
- Cooked and sliced sausages 4
- Mozzarella cheese, sliced in grater 112 g
- Cream 120 g

Directions:

1. Mix egg, butter and cream in a bowl.
2. Place the egg mix to your Ninja Foodi,
3. Spread the cheese and sausage slices on top of it.
4. Cook for 20 min at 345 °F/ °C /174 °C at "BAKE/ROAST" mode.
5. Serve and enjoy!

Nutrition Values Per Serving:
Calories: 180, Total fat: 12g, Carbohydrates: 4g, Protein: 12g

Cinnamon French Toast

Prep Time: 15 min
Cooking time: 10 min
Servings: 2
Ingredients:

- Beaten egg 2
- milk 59 ml
- Brown sugar 55 g
- Honey 21g
- Cinnamon 2.64 g
- Nutmeg 0.59 g
- Julienned whole meal bread, 4 slices

Directions:

1. Mix the ingredients in a bowl (except the bread).
2. Dip each strip of the bread in the mixture.
3. Now put the bread strips on the Ninja Foodi basket.
4. Place basket inside the pot and put the crisping lid cover.
5. Cook at 320 °F/ °C / 160 °C for almost 10 min in "Air Crisp" cooking mode.
6. Serve warm.

Nutrition Values Per Serving:
Calories: 295, Total fat: 6.1g, Carbohydrates: 50g, Protein: 11.9g

Mustard Rubbed Pork Chops

Prep Time: 10 min
Cooking time: 30 min
Servings: 4
Ingredients:

- Butter 28.4 g
- Dijon mustard   31.58 g
- Pork chops 4
- Salt and black pepper, to taste
- Fresh rosemary, chopped 3.35 g

Directions:

1. Cover pork chops with Dijon mustard, rosemary, salt, and pepper and marinate it for 2 hours.
2. Add butter and the marinated pork chops to your Ninja Foodi pot
3. Cook on Low-Medium Pressure for 30 min
4. Keep it for 10 min to release the pressure naturally.
5. Serve and enjoy!

Nutrition Values Per Serving:
Calories: 315, Total fat: 26g, Carbohydrates: 1g, Protein: 18g

Sweet Crepes

Prep Time: 5 min
Cooking time: 10 min
Servings: 4
Ingredients:

- Splenda 3.2 **g**
- Eggs 3
- Coconut flour 21g
- Heavy cream 120 **g**
- Coconut oil 43 ml melted and divided in 21.5 ml

Directions:
1. Mix 21.5 coconut oil, Splenda, eggs, salt very well in a proper bowl.
2. Add coconut flour while beating.
3. Pour the heavy cream and rest of the coconut oil and keep beating well
4. Set your Ninja Foodi to Sauté mode and add 1/4 of the mixture
5. Sauté for 2 min on each side. Repeat until all ingredients are used.
6. Enjoy!

Nutrition Values Per Serving:
Calories: 145, Total fat: 13g, Carbohydrates: 4g, Protein: 4g

Garlicky Potatoes

Cooking time: 20 min Servings: 2 Prep Time: 1 hour 10 min
Ingredients:

- Potatoes 2 (scrubbed, rinsed and diced)
- Olive oil 15 ml
- Salt to taste
- Garlic powder 0.82 **g**

Directions:
1. Put the potatoes in cold water. Soak for 45 min.
2. Dry the potatoes with a paper towel.
3. Toss in olive oil, salt and garlic powder.
4. Place in the Ninja Foodi basket. Seal the crisping lid. Select "Air Crisp" cooking mode.
5. Cook at 400 °F/ °C / 204°C for almost 20 min.
6. Half way through Flip the potatoes and cook the other side
7. Serve warm.

Nutrition Values Per Serving:
Calories: 208, Total fat: 7.2g, Carbohydrates: 34g, Protein: 3.6g

---

Seasoned Tofu Scramble

Servings: 4 Prep Time: 30 min Cooking time: 15 min
Ingredients:
- Olive oil 30 ml
- Soy sauce 28.3 **g**
- Onion, chopped 26 **g**
- Turmeric 3.18 g
- Onion powder 2.84 g
- Garlic powder 2.84 g
- Tofu 1 block (sliced into cubes)

Directions:
1. Mix the ingredients very well in a proper bowl except the tofu
2. Put the tofu in the mixture and soak it well for 5 min.
3. Place the tofu in the Ninja Foodi pot.
4. Seal the pot tightly and cover with the crisping lid.
5. Cook at 370 °F/ °C / 188°C for almost 15 min.
6. Place on a serving plate and Serve warm.

Nutrition Values Per Serving:
Calories: 90, Total fat: 8g, Carbohydrates: 3.2g, Protein: 2.7g

Chapter 2-Snacks and Appetizers Recipes

Buffalo Wings

Prep Time: 10 min Cooking time: 6 hours Servings: 4
Ingredients:

- 1 bottle of (12 ounces) hot pepper sauce
- 13.8 **g** melted ghee
- 1 tablespoon dried oregano
- 2 teaspoon garlic powder
- 1 teaspoon onion powder
- 5 pounds chicken wing sections

Directions:
1. Mix ghee, hot sauce, oregano, garlic powder, onion powder in a suitable bowl.
2. Add chicken wings and toss to coat.
3. Pour this mix into Ninja Foodi's insert and cook on "Slow Cook" mode with LOW heat for 6 hours.
4. Serve and enjoy!

Nutrition Values Per Serving:
Calories: 529, Total fat: 4g, Carbohydrates: 1g, Protein: 31g

Nutty Brussels Sprouts

Prep Time: 10 min Cooking time: 3 min Servings: 4
Ingredients:

- 1-pound Brussels sprouts
- 30g pine nuts
- 1 tablespoon olive oil
- 1 pomegranate
- ½ teaspoon salt
- 1 pepper, sliced in grater

Directions:
1. Remove outer leaves and trim the stems off the washed Brussels sprouts
2. Cut the largest ones in uniform halves
3. Add 240 mL water to the Ninja Foodi
4. Place steamer basket and add sprouts in the basket
5. Seal the lid and cook on "Pressure" mode at High for 3 min
6. Release the pressure naturally
7. Transfer the sprouts to the serving dish and dress with olive oil, pepper, and salt.
8. Sprinkle toasted pine nuts and pomegranate seeds!
9. Serve warm and enjoy!

Nutrition Values Per Serving:
Calories: 118, Total fat: 10g, Carbohydrates: 7g, Protein: 3g

Crispy Zucchini Fries

Prep Time: 10 min Cooking time: 10 min Servings: 4
Ingredients:

- 1-2 pounds of zucchini, sliced into 2 and ½ inch sticks
- Salt to taste
- 120g cream cheese
- 2 tbsp olive oil

Directions:

1. Add zucchini in a colander and season with salt, add cream cheese and mix
2. Add oil into your Ninja Foodie's pot and add Zucchini.
3. Lock the Air Crisping Lid and Set the temperature to 365 °F/ °C/ 185°C and timer to 10 min
4. Let it cook for 10 min and take the dish out once done, enjoy!

Nutrition Values Per Serving:
Calories: 374, Total fat: 36g, Carbohydrates: 6g, Protein: 7g

Bacon-Wrapped Drumsticks

Prep Time: 10 min Cooking time: 8 hours Servings: 6
Ingredients:

- 12 chicken drumsticks
- 12 slices thin-cut bacon

Directions:

1. Wrap each chicken drumsticks in bacon. Place drumsticks in your Ninja Foodi's insert.
2. Place lid and cook "Slow Cook" cooking mode with LOW heat for 8 hours.
3. Serve and enjoy!

Nutrition Values Per Serving:
Calories: 202, Total fat: 8g, Carbohydrates: 3g, Protein: 30g

Orange Cauliflower Salad

Prep Time: 10 min Cooking time: 10 min Servings: 4
Ingredients:

- 1 small-sized cauliflower, florets
- 1 Romanesco cauliflower, florets
- 1 pound of broccoli florets
- 2 seedless oranges, peeled and sliced

For vinaigrette

- 1 orange, juiced and zest
- 4 anchovies
- 1 hot pepper, sliced and chopped
- 1 tablespoon of capers
- 4 tablespoon of extra virgin olive oil
- Salt as needed
- Pepper as needed

Directions:

1. Add broccoli, cauliflower florets to your Ninja Foodi
2. Seal the lid and cook on "Pressure" mode at High for 7 min

3.   Once done, quick-release the pressure and remove the lid.
4.   Make the vinaigrette by mixing the hot pepper, anchovies, olive oil, capers, pepper, salt, and mix well.
5.   Strain the veggies out and mix with vinaigrette and the orange slices.
6.   Enjoy!

Nutrition Values Per Serving:
Calories: 163, Total fats: 11g, Carbs: 15g, Protein: 3g

Pickled Green Chili

Prep Time: 5 min Cooking time: 11 min Servings: 4
Ingredients:
- 1-pound green chilies
- 1 and ½ cups apple cider vinegar
- 1 teaspoon pickling salt
- 1 and ½ teaspoon sugar
- ¼ teaspoon garlic powder

Directions:
1.   Add the green Chilli ingredients to the Ninja Foodi's pot.
2.   Seal the lid and cook on "Pressure" mode at High for 11 min.
3.   Release the pressure naturally
4.   Spoon the mixture into jars and cover the slices with cooking liquid.
5.   Refrigerate the chilies overnight.
6.   Serve!

Nutrition Values Per Serving:
Calories: 3, Total fat: 0g, Carbohydrates: 0.8g, Protein: 0.1g

---

Chicken Stuffed Mushrooms

Prep Time: 10 min Cooking time: 20 min Servings: 4
Ingredients:
- 12 large fresh mushrooms, stems removed

Stuffing
- 140g chicken meat, cubed
- ½ pound, imitation crabmeat, flaked
- 453.6g butter
- Garlic powder to taste
- 2 garlic cloves, peeled and minced

Directions:
1.   Take a suitable skillet and place it over medium heat, add butter and let it heat
2.   Stir in meat chicken then sauté for 5 min.
3.   Add rest of the ingredients for stuffing and cook for 5 min
4.   Remove heat and let the chicken cool down. Divide filling into mushroom caps
5.   Place stuffed mushroom caps in your Crisping basket and transfer basket to Foodi
6.   Lock the Crisping Lid and cook on the "Air Crisp" mode for 10 min at 375 °F/ °C/191°C.
7.   Serve and enjoy!

Nutrition Values Per Serving:
Calories: 385, Total fat: 36g, Carbohydrates: 4g, Protein: 8g

Zucchini Gratin

Prep Time: 10 min Cooking time: 15 min Servings: 4
Ingredients:

- 2 zucchinis
- 1 tablespoon fresh parsley, chopped
- 2 tbsp bread crumbs
- 4 tbsp parmesan cheese, sliced in grater
- 1 tablespoon vegetable oil
- Salt and black pepper, to taste

Directions:
1. Pre-heat your Ninja Foodi to 300 °F/ 149 °C for almost 3 min
2. Slice zucchini lengthwise to get about 8 equal sizes pieces
3. Arrange the zucchini pieces in the Crisping Basket, with your skin side down.
4. Top each with parsley, bread crumbs, cheese, oil, salt, and pepper
5. Return basket to the Ninja Foodi Air Fryer's insert and cook for 15 min at 360°F/183°C.
6. Enjoy!

Nutrition Values Per Serving:
Calories: 481, Total fat: 11g, Carbohydrates: 10g, Protein: 7g

Cider dipped Chicken Thighs

Prep Time: 5 min Cooking time:6-8 hours Servings: 6
Ingredients:

- 3 pounds boneless chicken thighs, skinless
- 2 tbsp apple cider vinegar
- 175 g agave nectar
- 2 teaspoon garlic powder
- 2 teaspoon paprika
- 1 teaspoon Chilli powder
- 1 teaspoon red pepper flakes
- 1 teaspoon black pepper
- 2 teaspoon salt

Directions:
1. Mix paprika, red pepper flakes, Chilli powder, garlic pepper, salt, and pepper in a bowl.
2. Take another bowl and mix vinegar and agave nectar.
3. Use the seasoning mix to properly coat the chicken thigh.
4. Pour nectar, vinegar mix over chicken. Transfer the mix to Ninja Foodi
5. Lock the Ninja Foodi's lid and cook on "Slow Cook" cooking mode with low heat for 6-8 hours
6. Once done, unlock the lid. Drizzle the glaze on top and serve.
7. Enjoy!

Nutrition Values Per Serving:
Calories: 234, Total fat: 15g, Carbohydrates: 14g, Protein: 8g

Cheesy Chicken Parmesan

Prep Time: 10 min Cooking time: 20 min Servings: 4

Ingredients:

- 1 spaghetti squash
- 237 ml marinara sauce
- 1-pound chicken, cooked and cubed
- 16 ounces mozzarella

Directions:

1. Split the squash in halves and remove the seeds
2. Add 237 ml of water to the Ninja Foodi and place a trivet on top
3. Add the squash halves on the trivet. Seal the Ninja's lid and cook for 20 min at HIGH pressure
4. Do a quick release. Remove the squashes and shred them using a fork into spaghetti portions
5. Pour sauce over the squash and give it a nice mix
6. Top them with the cubed chicken and top with mozzarella
7. Broil for 1-2 min and broil until the cheese has melted.
8. Serve warm.

Nutrition Values Per Serving:

Calories: 127, Total fats: 8g, Carbs:11g, Protein:5g

Cider Dipped Chili

Prep Time: 10 min Cooking time: 11 min Servings: 4

Ingredients:

- 1-pound green chilies
- 1 and ½ cups apple cider vinegar
- 1 teaspoon pickling salt
- 1 and ½ teaspoon date paste
- ¼ teaspoon garlic powder

Directions:

1. Add the above-mentioned ingredients to the Ninja Foodi's insert.
2. Seal the lid and cook on "Pressure" mode at High for 10 min
3. Release the pressure naturally
4. Spoon the mix into washed jars and cover the slices with a bit of cooking liquid
5. Add vinegar to submerge the chilly.
6. Enjoy!

Nutrition Values Per Serving:

Calories: 3.1, Total fat: 0g, Carbohydrates: 0.6g, Protein: 0.1g

Crispy Beet Chips

Prep Time: 10 min Cooking time: 8 hours Servings: 8

Ingredients:

- ½ beet, peeled and sliced

Directions:

1. Arrange beet slices in a single layer in the Crisper basket of Ninja Foodi.
2. Place the basket into the Ninja Foodi's pot and close the crisping lid.
3. Press the Dehydrate button and let it dehydrate for 8 hours at 135 °F/ 58 °C.
4. Once the dehydrating is done, remove the basket from the pot.

5.   Serve.
Nutrition Values Per Serving:
Calories: 35, Total fat: 0g, Carbohydrates: 8g, Protein: 1g

Cheesy Mushroom Appetizer

Prep Time: 10 min Cooking time: 20 min Servings: 6
Ingredients:

- 24 mushrooms, caps and stems diced
- 235 **g** cheddar cheese, shredded
- ½ orange bell pepper, diced
- ½ onion, diced
- 4 bacon slices, diced
- 123 **g** sour cream

Directions:
1.   Set your Ninja Foodie to Sauté mode and add mushroom stems, onion, bacon, bell pepper and Sauté for 5 min.
2.   Add 1 cup cheese, sour cream and cook for 2 min.
3.   Stuff mushrooms with cheese and vegetable mixture and top with cheddar cheese
4.   Transfer them to your Crisping Basket and lock the Air Crisping lid.
5.   Cook on "Air Crisp" mode for 8 min at 350 °F/ 177 °C.
6.   Serve and enjoy!

Nutrition Values Per Serving:
Calories: 288, Total fat: 6g, Carbohydrates: 3g, Protein: 25g

Saucy Chicken Thighs

Prep Time: 10 min Cooking time: 5-7 hours Servings: 4
Ingredients:

- 3 pounds boneless, skinless chicken thighs
- 48g low-sodium chicken broth
- 2 cups cherry tomatoes, halved
- 4 garlic cloves, minced
- 2 teaspoon garlic salt
- ¼ teaspoon ground white pepper
- 2 tbsp fresh basil, chopped
- 2 tbsp fresh oregano, chopped

Directions:
1.   Add the chicken and all the listed ingredients to your Ninja Foodi and mix gently.
2.   Lock the Ninja Foodi's lid and cook on "Slow Cook" mode with Low Heat for 5-7 hours.
3.   Serve and enjoy!

Creamy Fudge Meal

Prep Time: 10 min + chill times Cooking time: 10-20 min Servings: 20
Ingredients:

- ½ teaspoon organic vanilla extract
- 231g heavy whip cream
- 2 ounces butter, soft
- 2 ounces 70% dark chocolate, finely chopped

Directions:
1. Set your Ninja Foodi to Sauté mode and add vanilla, heavy cream. Sauté for 5 min
2. Add butter and chocolate and Sauté for 2 min. Transfer to serving the dish
3. Chill for few hours and enjoy!

Nutrition Values Per Serving:
Calories: 292, Total fat: 26g, Carbohydrates: 8g, Protein: 5g

Bacon with Bok Choy

Prep Time: 10 min Cooking time:3 min Servings: 4
Ingredients:

- ½ tbsp fresh lemon juice
- 1 medium ripe avocado, peeled and pitted, chopped
- 6 organic eggs, boiled, peeled and cut half
- Salt to taste
- 34g fresh watercress, trimmed

Directions:
1. Place the Ninja's steamer basket at the bottom of the Ninja Foodi's insert.
2. Add water to the insert and put the watercress in the basket.
3. Lock the Ninja Foodi's lid and pressure cook for 3 min
4. Quick-release pressure, then remove the lid.
5. Allow the boiled eggs to cool, peel and cut them in half.
6. Remove egg yolk and transfer to a suitable bowl
7. Add watercress, avocado, lemon juice, salt, and mash well
8. Place egg whites in serving the dish and fill whites with watercress, mix well.
9. Enjoy!

Nutrition Values Per Serving:
Calories: 132, Total fat: 10g, Carbohydrates: 3g, Protein: 6g

Mexican Cheese Frittata

Prep Time: 10 min Cooking time: 25 min Servings: 4
Ingredients:

- 4 whole eggs
- 242g half and half
- 10 ounces canned green chilies

- ½ -1 teaspoon salt
- ½ teaspoon ground cumin
- 83g Mexican blend shredded cheese
- 4g cilantro, chopped

Directions:
1. Take a suitable bowl and beat eggs and a half and half
2. Add diced green chilis, salt, cumin and 41.5 g of shredded cheese
3. Pour the mixture into 6 inches greased metal pan and cover with foil
4. Add 473 ml of water to the Ninja Foodi.
5. Place trivet into the Ninja Foodi's pot and place the pan in the trivet
6. Seal the lid and cook on "Pressure" mode at High for 20 min
7. Release the pressure naturally over 10 min
8. Scatter half a cup of the cheese on top of your quiche.
9. Enjoy!

Nutrition Values Per Serving:
Calories: 257, Total fat: 19g, Carbohydrates: 6g, Protein:14g

Braised Kale Salad

Prep Time: 5 min Cooking time: 8 min Servings: 4
Ingredients:

- 10 ounces kale, chopped
- 1 tablespoon ghee
- 1 medium onion, sliced
- 3 medium carrots, cut into half-inch pieces
- 5 garlic cloves, peeled and chopped
- 100 ml chicken broth
- Fresh ground pepper
- Vinegar as needed
- ½ teaspoon red pepper flakes

Directions:
1. Set your pot to Sauté mode and add ghee, allow the ghee to melt
2. Add chopped onion and carrots and Sauté for a while
3. Add garlic and Sauté for a while. Pile the kale on top
4. Pour chicken broth and season with pepper
5. Seal the lid and cook on "Pressure" mode at High for 8 min
6. Release the pressure naturally over 10 min and remove the lid.
7. Add vinegar and sprinkle a bit more pepper flakes.
8. Enjoy!

Nutrition Values Per Serving:
Calories: 41, Total fat: 2g, Carbohydrates: 5g, Protein: 2g

Chapter 3-Pork, Beef & Lamb Recipes

Beef Jerky

Prep Time: 10 min Cooking Time: 4 hours Servings: 4
Ingredients:

- ½ pound beef, julienned
- 2 tbsp Worcestershire sauce
- 1 teaspoon onion powder
- 120 ml of soy sauce
- 1/2 teaspoon garlic powder
- 1 teaspoon salt
- 2 teaspoon black pepper

Directions:
1. Take a large-sized Ziplock bag and add all the ingredients.
2. Seal and refrigerate the beef strips overnight.
3. Place the strips on a dehydrator tray and place them in the Ninja Foodi's pot.
4. Cook for 4 hours at 135 °F/58 °C on Dehydrate Mode.
5. Serve and enjoy!

Nutrition Values Per Serving:
Calories: 62, Total fat: 7g, Carbohydrates: 2g, Protein: 31g

Mexican Beef Short Ribs

Prep Time: 10 min Cooking Time: 35 min Servings: 4
Ingredients:

- 2 and ½ pounds boneless beef short ribs
- 1 tablespoon Chilli powder
- 1 and ½ teaspoon salt
- 1 tablespoon fat
- 1 medium onion, thinly sliced
- 1 tablespoon tomato sauce
- 6 garlic cloves, peeled and smashed
- 130g roasted tomato salsa
- 126ml bone broth
- Fresh black pepper
- 8g cilantro, minced
- 2 radishes, sliced

Directions:
1. Mix beef, salt, Chilli powder in a suitable bowl.
2. Set the temperature Ninja Foodi to Sauté mode, add butter to melt.
3. Add garlic, tomato paste, then sauté for 30 seconds
4. Add beef stock and fish sauce on top.
5. Lock the Ninja Foodi's lid and cook on "Pressure" mode on HIGH for 35 min.
6. Naturally, release pressure, then remove the lid.
7. Enjoy!

Nutrition Values Per Serving:

Calories: 308, Total fat: 18g, Carbohydrates: 21g, Protein: 38g

Adobo Beef Steak

Prep Time: 5 min Cooking Time: 25 min Servings: 4

Ingredients:

- 473 ml of water
- 8 steaks, cubed, 28 ounces pack
- Black pepper to taste
- 1 and ¾ teaspoon adobo seasoning
- 1 can (8 ounces) tomato sauce
- 60 **g** green pitted olives
- 2 tbsp brine
- 1 small red pepper
- 1/2 a medium onion, sliced

Directions:

1. Chop onions and peppers into 1/4-inch strips
2. Season the beef with pepper and adobo.
3. Add to the Ninja Foodi's insert, then add remaining ingredients and Close the Ninja's lid.
4. Cook on "Pressure" mode for 25 min on HIGH.
5. Release pressure naturally, then remove the lid.
6. Serve and enjoy!

Nutrition Values Per Serving:

Calories: 429, Total fat: 24g, Carbohydrates: 11g, Protein: 31g

Tomato Beef Stew

Prep Time: 11 min Cooking Time: 10 min Servings: 4

Ingredients:

- 1-pound beef roast
- 950 ml beef broth
- 2 tomatoes, chopped
- 1/2 white onion, chopped
- 3 garlic cloves, chopped
- 1 carrot, chopped
- 2 celery stalks, chopped
- 1/4 teaspoon salt
- 1/8 teaspoon black pepper

Directions:

1. Add beef roast along with all ingredients to your Ninja Foodi's inset.
2. Cover the Foodi's lid and seal it for pressure cooking.
3. Cook on "Pressure" mode for 10 min on HIGH.
4. Release pressure naturally, then remove the lid.
5. Serve and enjoy!

Nutrition Values Per Serving:

Calories: 529, Total fat: 4g, Carbohydrates: 1g, Protein: 31g

Smothered Pork Chops

Prep Time: 10 min Cooking Time: 28 min Servings: 4
Ingredients:

- 6 ounce of boneless pork loin chops
- 1 tablespoon of paprika
- 1 teaspoon of garlic powder
- 1 teaspoon of onion powder
- 1 teaspoon of black pepper
- 1 teaspoon of salt
- 1/4 teaspoon of cayenne pepper
- 2 tablespoon of coconut oil
- 1/2 of a sliced medium onion
- 6-ounce baby Bella mushrooms, sliced
- 1 tablespoon of butter
- 120 **g** of whip cream
- 1/4 teaspoon of xanthan gum
- 1 tablespoon parsley, chopped

Directions:

1. Mix garlic powder, paprika, onion powder, black pepper, salt, and cayenne pepper
2. Rub the seasoning all over the meat
3. Reserve the remaining spice mixture
4. Set your Ninja Foodi to Sauté mode and add coconut oil to heat.
5. Brown the chops 3 min per sides.
6. Add sliced onion to the base of your Ninja Foodi along with mushrooms.
7. Top with the browned pork chops, then seal the lid to cook for 10 min on High pressure.
8. Release the pressure and remove the lid. Transfer the pork chops to a plate.
9. Set your Ninja Foodi to Sauté mode and whisk in remaining spices mix, heavy cream, and butter
10. Sprinkle 1/4 teaspoon of xanthan gum and stir
11. Simmer for 3-5 min and remove the heat
12. Serve warm with the pork.

Nutrition Values Per Serving:
Calories: 481, Total fat: 32g, Carbohydrates: 6g, Protein: 39g

Beef Pork Chili

Prep Time: 10 min Cooking Time: 35 min Servings: 4
Ingredients:

- 1-pound ground beef
- 1-pound ground pork
- 3 tomatillos, chopped
- 1 teaspoon garlic powder
- 1 jalapeno pepper
- 1 tablespoon ground cumin
- 1 tablespoon Chilli powder
- Salt as needed

Directions:

1. Set your Ninja Foodi to Sauté mode and add beef and pork. Sauté until brown.
2. Add onion, garlic, tomatillo, tomato paste, jalapeno, cumin, water, Chilli powder, and mix well.
3. Seal the lid and cook on "Pressure" mode on High for 35 min.

4.   Release the Pressure naturally, then remove the lid.
5.   Serve and enjoy!

Nutrition Values Per Serving:
Calories: 325, Total fat: 23g, Carbohydrates: 6g, Protein: 20g

---

Kale Sausage Soup

Prep Time: 5-10 min Cooking Time: 10 min Servings: 4

Ingredients:

- 1/2 diced onion
- 475 ml chicken broth
- 1-pound chopped sausage roll
- 1 tablespoon olive oil
- 2 cup almond milk
- 45 **g** parmesan cheese
- 201g chopped kale fresh
- 28-ounce tomatoes, crushed
- 1 tablespoon minced garlic
- 1 teaspoon oregano, dried
- 1/4 teaspoon salt

Directions:

1.   Preheat your Ninja Foodi on "SEAR/SAUTÉ" mode.
2.   Add the sausage and stir-cook to brown evenly.
3.   Stir in spices, onions, kale, tomatoes, milk, and chicken broth, then mix well.
4.   Select "PRESSURE" mode with high pressure level and seal the lid.
5.   Naturally, release inside pressure for about 8-10 min.
6.   Serve warm with the cheese on top.
7.   Enjoy.

Nutrition Values Per Serving:
Calories: 162, Total fat: 11g, Carbohydrates: 2g, Protein: 19g

---

Jamaican Pork Meal

Prep Time: 10 min Cooking Time: 30 min Servings: 4

Ingredients:

- 120g beef stock
- 1 tablespoon olive oil
- 62g Jamaican jerk spice blend
- 4 ounces of pork shoulder

Directions:

1.   Rub roast with olive oil and spice blend
2.   Set your Ninja Foodi to Sauté mode and add meat, brown all sides
3.   Pour beef broth and seal the lid.
4.   Cook on "Pressure" cook mode at High for 30 min.
5.   Release the pressure completely then remove the lid and shred the meat.
6.   Serve warm.

Nutrition Values Per Serving:
Calories: 308, Total fat: 18g, Carbohydrates: 5g, Protein: 31g

Mustard Glazed Pork

Prep Time: 10 min Cooking Time: 30 min Servings: 4

Ingredients:

- 2 tbsp ghee
- 2 tbsp Dijon mustard
- 4 pork chops
- Salt and black pepper, to taste
- 1 tablespoon fresh rosemary, chopped

Directions:

1. Take a suitable bowl and add pork chops, cover with Dijon mustard and carefully sprinkle rosemary, salt, and pepper
2. Let it marinate for 2 hours
3. Add ghee and marinated pork chops to your Ninja Foodi pot
4. Lock the Ninja Foodi's lid and cook on Low-Medium Pressure for 30 min
5. Release pressure naturally over 10 min
6. Serve and enjoy.

Nutrition Values Per Serving:

Calories: 315, Total fat: 26g, Carbohydrates: 1g, Protein: 18g

Onion Pork Chops

Prep Time: 10 min Cooking Time: 20 min Servings: 4

Ingredients:

- 4 pork chops
- 10 ounces French Onion Soup
- 123 g sour cream
- 10 ounces chicken broth

Directions:

1. Add pork chops and broth to your Ninja Foodi's insert.
2. Lock the Ninja Foodi's lid and cook on "Pressure" mode at High for 12 min
3. Release pressure naturally over 10 min, then remove the lid.
4. Whisk sour cream and French Onion Soup and pour mixture over pork
5. Set your Ninja Foodi to Sauté mode and cook for 6-8 min more
6. Serve and enjoy!

Nutrition Values Per Serving:

Calories: 356, Total fat: 26g, Carbohydrates: 7g, Protein: 21g

Ranch Beef Roast

Prep Time: 10 min Cooking Time: 60 min Servings: 4

Ingredients:

- 3 pounds beef roast
- 1 tablespoon olive oil
- 2 tbsp ranch dressing
- 1 jar pepper rings, with juices
- 8 tbsp butter
- 237 ml of water

Directions:

1. Set your Ninja Foodi to Sauté mode and add 1 tablespoon of oil
2. Once the oil is hot, add roast and sear on both sides.
3. Add water, reserved juice, seasoning mix, and pepper rings on top of the beef.
4. Seal the lid and cook on "Pressure" mode on HIGH for 60 min.
5. Release the pressure naturally over 10 min
6. Cut the beef with salad sheers and enjoy with pureed cauliflower
7. Enjoy!

Nutrition Values Per Serving:
Calories: 365, Total fat: 18g, Carbohydrates: 12g, Protein: 16g

Indian Beef Meal

Prep Time: 10 min Cooking Time: 20 min Servings: 4

Ingredients:

- ½ yellow onion, chopped
- 1 tablespoon olive oil
- 2 garlic cloves, minced
- 1 jalapeno pepper, chopped
- 236ml cherry tomatoes, quartered
- 1 teaspoon fresh lemon juice
- 1-2 pounds grass-fed ground beef
- 1-2 pounds fresh collard greens, trimmed and chopped

Spices

- 1 teaspoon cumin, ground
- ½ teaspoon ginger, ground
- 1 teaspoon coriander, ground
- ½ teaspoon fennel seeds, ground
- ½ teaspoon cinnamon, ground
- Salt and black pepper, to taste
- ½ teaspoon turmeric, ground

Directions:

1. Set your Ninja Foodi to Sauté mode, add garlic and onion, then Sauté for 3 min.
2. Add Jalapeno pepper, beef, spices and stir well.
3. Lock the Ninja Foodi's lid and cook on "Pressure" mode on MEDIUM for 15 min.
4. Release pressure naturally and remove the lid.
5. Add tomatoes and collard, sauté for 3 min
6. Stir in lemon juice, salt, and black pepper, then mix well.
7. Serve and enjoy!

Nutrition Values Per Serving:
Calories: 409, Total fat: 16g, Carbohydrates: 5g, Protein: 56g

New York Steak

Prep Time: 10 min Cooking Time: 9 min Servings: 4

Ingredients:

- 24 ounces NY strip steak
- ½ teaspoon black pepper
- 1 teaspoon salt

Directions:

1. Add steaks on a metal trivet, place it on your Ninja Foodi
2. For seasoning, add salt and black pepper on top.
3. Add 1 cup water to the Ninja Foodi's pot.
4. Cover the Foodi's lid and seal it for pressure cooking.
5. Cook on "Pressure" mode for 1 minute on HIGH.
6. Release pressure naturally, then remove the lid.
7. Place Air-crisp lid and cook on the "Air Crisp" mode for 8 min for a medium-steak.
8. Serve and enjoy!

Nutrition Values Per Serving:
Calories: 503, Total fat: 46g, Carbohydrates: 1g, Protein: 46g

---

Cheesy Beef Meatloaf

Prep Time: 5-10 min Cooking Time: 70 min Servings: 6
Ingredients:

- 56.2 **g** tomato puree or crushed tomatoes
- 1-pound lean ground beef
- 26 **g** onion, chopped
- 2 garlic cloves, minced
- 75g green bell pepper, chopped
- 2 eggs, beaten
- 235g cheddar cheese, sliced in grater
- 90 **g** spinach, chopped
- 1 teaspoon dried thyme, crushed
- 792g mozzarella cheese, sliced in grater
- Black pepper to taste

Directions:

1. Grease a baking pan with cooking spray.
2. Mix all the listed ingredients except cheese and spinach.
3. Place the prepared mixture over the wax paper; top it with spinach, cheese, and roll it to make a meatloaf.
4. Remove wax paper and add the rolled meatloaf to the baking pan.
5. Add water to the Ninja Foodi's pot and place a reversible rack inside the pot.
6. Place the pan on the rack.
7. Select "BAKE/ROAST" mode and adjust the 380 °F/ 193 °C.
8. Then, Set the temperature timer to 70 min and hit "STOP/START."
9. Serve warm.

Nutrition Values Per Serving:
Calories: 426, Total fat: 17g, Carbohydrates: 5.5g, Protein: 49g

---

Lemon Pork Cutlets

Prep Time: 10 min Cooking Time: 5 min Servings: 4
Ingredients:

- 112ml hot sauce
- 118 ml cup of water
- 2 tbsp butter
- 79 ml lemon juice
- 1-pound pork cutlets
- ½ teaspoon paprika

Directions:
1. Add pork cutlets and all other listed ingredients to the Ninja Foodi.
2. Lock the Ninja Foodi's lid and cook on "Pressure" mode at High for 5 min.
3. Now release the cooker's pressure naturally for 10 min, then remove the lid.
4. Gently mix and serve warm.

Nutrition Values Per Serving:
Calories: 414, Total fat: 21g, Carbohydrates: 3g, Protein: 50g

Beef Meatballs with Marinara Sauce

Prep Time: 10 min Cooking Time: 11 min Servings: 4
Ingredients:

- 300 **g** ground beef
- 1 egg, beaten
- 1 teaspoon taco seasoning
- 1 tablespoon sugar-free marinara sauce
- 1 teaspoon garlic, minced
- ½ teaspoon salt

Directions:
1. Mix ground beef with egg, taco seasoning and the rest of the ingredients in a bowl.
2. Make golf-ball sized meatballs out of this mixture and put them in a single layer in the Air fryer's Basket.
3. Cover the crisping lid and cook on "Air Crisp" mode for 11 min at 350 °F/177 °C.
4. Serve immediately and enjoy!

Nutrition Values Per Serving:
Calories: 205, Total fat: 12g, Carbohydrates: 2g, Protein: 19g

Saucy Lamb Roast

Prep Time: 10 min Cooking Time: 60 min Servings: 4
Ingredients:

- 2 pounds lamb roasted Wegmans
- 241 **g** beef broth

- 112 **g** onion soup
- Salt and black pepper, to taste

Directions:

1. Place your lamb roast in your Ninja Foodi pot
2. Add beef broth, onion soup, salt and black pepper.
3. Cover the Foodi's lid and seal it for pressure cooking.
4. Cook on "Pressure" mode for 55 min on HIGH.
5. Release pressure naturally, then remove the lid.
6. Serve and enjoy!

Nutrition Values Per Serving:
Calories: 211, Total fat: 7g, Carbohydrates: 2g, Protein: 30g

Herbed Pork Chops

Prep Time: 10 min Cooking Time: 30 min Servings: 4
Ingredients:

- 2 tbsp ghee
- 2 tbsp Dijon mustard
- 4 pork chops
- Salt and black pepper, to taste
- 1 tablespoon fresh rosemary, chopped

Directions:

1. Take a suitable bowl and add pork chops, cover with Dijon mustard and carefully sprinkle rosemary, salt, and black pepper.
2. Let it marinate for 2 hours
3. Add ghee and marinated pork chops to your Ninja Foodi pot.
4. Cover the Foodi's lid and seal it for pressure cooking.
5. Cook on "Pressure" mode for 30 min on Low.
6. Release pressure naturally, then remove the lid.
7. Serve and enjoy!

Nutrition Values Per Serving:
Calories: 315, Total fat: 26g, Carbohydrates: 1g, Protein: 18g

Chapter 4-Chicken and Poultry Recipes

Chicken Cauliflower Pilaf

Prep Time: 15 min Cooking time: 6 min Servings: 10
Ingredients:

- 113 **g** cauliflower rice
- 7 ounces chicken breasts, boneless
- 1 teaspoon salt
- 4 ounces mushrooms
- 1 tablespoon olive oil
- 1 white onion
- 1 tablespoon oregano
- 4 ounces raisins
- 5 ounces kale
- 7 ounces green beans
- 288 g chicken stock
- 2 tbsp oyster sauce

Directions:
1. Slice the mushrooms and place them into the Ninja Foodi.
2. Chop the chicken breasts into medium-sized pieces and add them to the Ninja Foodi.
3. Peel the onion and dice it. Chop the kale and green beans.
4. Transfer the vegetables to the Ninja Foodi.
5. Top the mixture with olive oil, salt, oregano, raisins, and chicken stock.
6. Set the temperature Ninja Foodi to" Pressure" mode and stir well.
7. Add the cauliflower rice and close the Ninja Foodi's lid.
8. Cook on "Pressure" mode for 6 min at High.
9. Once it is done, release the cooker's pressure then remove the Ninja Foodi's lid.
10. Let the pilaf rest and stir well before serving.

Nutrition Values Per Serving:
Calories: 111, Total fat: 3.2g, Fiber: 2.1g, Carbohydrates: 14.4g, Protein: 7.8g

Coconut Dipped Chicken Strips

Prep Time: 10 min Cooking time: 12 min Servings: 8
Ingredients:

- 140 g coconut
- 4 tbsp butter
- 1 teaspoon salt
- 45 g flour
- ½ teaspoon Sugar
- ¼ teaspoon red Chilli flakes
- 1 teaspoon onion powder
- 15 ounces boneless chicken breast

Directions:

1. Cut the boneless chicken breast into the strips, sprinkle it with the salt and Chilli flakes, and stir.
2. Mix the coconut, flour, sugar, and onion powder in a suitable mixing bowl and stir well.
3. Set the temperature Ninja Foodi to" Sauté" mode.
4. Add the butter into the Ninja Foodi and cook for 2 min.
5. Dip the chicken strips in the coconut mixture well and transfer the chicken strips into the Ninja Foodi.
6. Sauté the dish for 10 min on both sides.
7. When the chicken is golden brown, remove the chicken strips to a plate.
8. Let the dish rest briefly and serve.

Nutrition Values Per Serving:
Calories: 197, Total fat: 13.7g, Fiber: 1g, Carbohydrates: 2.3g, Protein: 16.6g

Seasoned Whole Chicken

Prep Time: 15 min Cooking time: 30 min Servings: 9
Ingredients:
- 2 pounds whole chicken, wash and cleaned
- 1 tablespoon salt
- 1 teaspoon black pepper
- 1 tablespoon olive oil
- 1 teaspoon butter
- 1 teaspoon fresh rosemary
- 1 lemon
- 1 tablespoon sugar
- 237 ml of water
- 1 teaspoon coriander, chopped
- ½ teaspoon cayenne pepper
- ¼ teaspoon turmeric

Directions:
1. Mix the salt, black pepper, fresh rosemary, sugar, coriander, cayenne pepper, and turmeric in a suitable mixing bowl.
2. Rub the chicken with the spice mixture.
3. Sprinkle the chicken with olive oil. Set the temperature Ninja Foodi to" Pressure" mode.
4. Pour the water into the Ninja Foodi and place the stuffed whole chicken.
5. Seal the lid and cook for 30 min at HI pressure.
6. Once it is done, release the cooker's pressure and open the Ninja Foodi's lid.
7. Remove the prepared chicken from the Ninja Foodi and let it rest.
8. Cut the cooked chicken into pieces and serve warm.

Nutrition Values Per Serving:
Calories: 217, Total fat: 9.5g, Fiber: 0.3g, Carbohydrates: 2.3g, Protein: 29.3g

Mexican Chicken with Salsa

Prep Time: 13 min Cooking time: 15 min Servings: 6
Ingredients:
- 260 g of salsa
- 1 teaspoon paprika
- 1 teaspoon salt
- 2 tbsp minced garlic
- 15 ounces boneless chicken breast

- 1 teaspoon oregano

Directions:
1. Mix the paprika, salt, minced garlic, and oregano in a suitable mixing bowl and stir.
2. Chop the boneless chicken breast and sprinkle it with the spice mixture.
3. Set the temperature Ninja Foodi to" Pressure" mode.
4. Transfer the chicken mixture into the Ninja Foodi, add the salsa, and mix well using a wooden spoon.
5. Close the Ninja's lid and cook for 15 min.
6. Once it is done, release the cooker's pressure and open the Ninja Foodi's lid.
7. Transfer the cooked chicken with salsa to a serving bowl.

Nutrition Values Per Serving:
Calories: 206, Total fat: 10.3g, Fiber: 3g, Carbohydrates: 20.49g, Protein: 9g

---

Chicken Mushrooms Rice

Prep Time: 15 min Cooking time: 35 min Servings: 8
Ingredients:

- 113 g cauliflower rice
- 600 ml chicken stock
- 1 tablespoon salt
- 2 tbsp butter
- 2 big carrots, peeled and chopped
- 1 white onion, chopped
- 8 ounces mushrooms, chopped
- 1 tablespoon dry dill
- 1 tablespoon cream
- 1 teaspoon rosemary
- 1 teaspoon ground cumin
- 1 teaspoon paprika
- 1 teaspoon oregano
- 1 tablespoon cilantro, chopped
- 1 teaspoon chives, chopped
- 1-pound chicken breast, diced

Directions:
1. Mix the rosemary, cream, black pepper, oregano, paprika, cilantro, and chives in a suitable mixing bowl.
2. Add chopped chicken breast to the cream mixture and mix well.
3. Set the temperature Ninja Foodi to" Sauté" mode. Stir in butter to melt.
4. Add the sliced vegetables and sauté for 10 min.
5. Add the creamy chicken mixture, chicken stock, and cauliflower rice.
6. Close the Ninja's lid and cook on" Manual" mode for 25 min.
7. Once done, remove the lid and serve warm.

Nutrition Values Per Serving:
Calories: 121, Total fat: 4.8g, Fiber: 1.6g, Carbohydrates: 5.7g, Protein: 14g

Creamy Pulled Chicken

Prep Time: 15 min Cooking time: 25 min Servings: 7
Ingredients:

- 231 g cream
- 200 ml chicken stock
- 1 tablespoon garlic sauce
- 1 tablespoon minced garlic
- 1 teaspoon nutmeg
- 1 teaspoon salt
- 12 ounces of chicken breasts
- 1 tablespoon lemon juice

Directions:
1. Mix the nutmeg and salt and stir well.
2. Sprinkle the chicken breasts with the salt mixture, coating them well.
3. Set the temperature Ninja Foodi to" Pressure" mode.
4. Place the chicken into the Ninja Foodi.
5. Add chicken stock, minced garlic, and cream, stir well and Close the Ninja's lid.
6. Cook on "Pressure" mode at High for 25 min.
7. Once it is done, release the cooker's pressure and open the Ninja Foodi's lid.
8. Transfer the chicken to a mixing bowl.
9. Shred the meat using a fork. Add the garlic sauce, mix well, and serve.

Nutrition Values Per Serving:
Calories: 169, Total fat: 11.8g, Fiber: 0g, Carbohydrates: 3.32g, Protein: 12g

Chicken Noodle Soup

Prep Time: 15 min Cooking time: 29 min Servings: 9
Ingredients:
- 6 ounces Shirataki noodles
- 1,893 ml of water
- 1 carrot
- 1 tablespoon peanut oil
- 1 yellow onion
- ½ tablespoon salt
- 3 ounces celery stalk
- 1 teaspoon black pepper
- ½ lemon
- 1 teaspoon minced garlic
- 10 ounces chicken breast

Directions:
1. Peel the carrot and onion and dice them.
2. Cut the chicken breast into halves.
3. Set the temperature Ninja Foodi to" Pressure" mode.
4. Pour the peanut oil into the Ninja Foodi and preheat it for 1 minute.
5. Add the onion and carrot and stir well; cook it for 5 min, stirring constantly.
6. Add 4 cups of water and chicken breast.

7. Close the Ninja's lid and cook the dish on" Pressure" mode for 10 min.
8. Once it is done, remove the chicken from the Ninja Foodi and shred it.
9. Return the shredded chicken to the Ninja Foodi and Close the Ninja's lid.
10. Cook the dish for 7 min. Add 4 cups of water and Shirataki noodles.
11. Close the Ninja's lid and cook the dish on "Pressure" mode for 7 min.
12. When the soup is done, transfer it from the Ninja Foodi to the serving bowls.

Nutrition Values Per Serving:
Calories: 64, Total fat: 2.3g, Fiber: 2.7g, Carbohydrates: 2.6g, Protein: 7.2g

Italian Chicken Breasts

Prep Time: 10 min Cooking time: 25 min Servings: 6
Ingredients:

- 13-ounce Italian-style salad dressing
- 1 teaspoon butter
- 1-pound chicken breast, skinless

Directions:
1. Chop the chicken breasts roughly and place them in a suitable mixing bowl.
2. Sprinkle the chopped meat with the Italian-style salad dressing and mix well using your hands.
3. Let the chicken marinate breast for 1 hour in your refrigerator.
4. Set the temperature Ninja Foodi to" Pressure" mode.
5. Add the butter into the Ninja Foodi.
6. Add marinated chicken breast and cook for 25 min.
7. Once it is done, remove the chicken from the Ninja Foodi and let it rest briefly.
8. Transfer the dish to a serving plate.

Nutrition Values Per Serving:
Calories: 283, Total fat: 20.6g, Fiber: 0g, Carbohydrates: 7.45g, Protein: 16g

Chicken Thigh Puttanesca

Prep Time: 15 min Cooking time: 25 min Servings: 8
Ingredients:

- 1 ½ pounds chicken thighs
- 112 g tomato paste
- 2 tbsp capers
- 1 teaspoon salt
- 1/2 teaspoon black-eyed peas
- 3 garlic cloves
- 3 tbsp olive oil
- 4 ounces black olives
- 1 tablespoon fresh basil, chopped
- 118 ml of water

Directions:
1. Set the temperature Ninja Foodi to" Sauté" mode.

2. Pour the olive oil into the Ninja Foodi and preheat it for 1 minute.
3. Place the chicken thighs into the Ninja Foodi and sauté the chicken for 5 min.
4. Once the chicken thighs are golden, remove them from the Ninja Foodi and keep aside.
5. Put the tomato paste, capers, olives, black-eyed peas, and basil into the Ninja Foodi.
6. Peel the garlic and slice it. Add the sliced garlic to the Ninja Foodi mixture.
7. Add the salt and water. Stir the mixture well and sauté it for 3 min.
8. Add the chicken thighs and Close the Ninja's lid.
9. Cook the dish on" Pressure" mode for 17 min.
10. Once it is done, open the Ninja Foodi's lid and transfer the dish to the serving bowl.

Nutrition Values Per Serving:
Calories: 170, Total fat: 8.8g, Fiber: 1g, Carbohydrates: 4.48g, Protein: 18g

Creamy Stuffed Chicken Breast

Prep Time: 10 min Cooking time: 20 min Servings: 7
Ingredients:
- 6.7 g basil
- 3 ounces dry tomatoes
- 1-pound chicken breast
- 1 tablespoon olive oil
- 3 ounces dill
- 1 teaspoon paprika
- ½ teaspoon ground ginger
- 1 teaspoon salt
- ½ teaspoon ground coriander
- ½ teaspoon cayenne pepper
- 2 tbsp lemon juice
- 61 g sour cream

Directions:
1. Wash the basil and chop it. Chop the dried tomatoes.
2. Mix the chopped ingredients in a suitable mixing bowl and sprinkle with the paprika and ground ginger and stir well.
3. Pound the prepared chicken breast with a mallet to flatten them.
4. Rub the chicken breast with the dill, salt, ground coriander, cayenne pepper, and lemon juice. Fill the chicken breast with the chopped basil mixture.
5. Set the temperature Ninja Foodi to" Steam" mode. Spray the Ninja Foodi with olive oil. Spread the stuffed chicken breast with sour cream.
6. Close the chicken breasts with toothpicks and place them in the Ninja Foodi.
7. Close the Ninja Foodi's lid and cook for 20 min.
8. Once it is done, open the Ninja Foodi's lid and remove the chicken breast.
9. Remove the toothpicks, slice the stuffed chicken breast, and serve.

Nutrition Values Per Serving:
Calories: 179, Total fat: 9.4g, Fiber: 2g, Carbohydrates: 8.89g, Protein: 16g

Thai Chicken

Prep Time: 10 min Cooking time: 35 min Servings: 8
Ingredients:

- 14 ounces boneless chicken breast
- 1 teaspoon black pepper
- 1 teaspoon paprika
- 1 teaspoon turmeric
- 3 tbsp fish sauce
- ½ teaspoon curry
- 1 teaspoon salt
- 3 tbsp butter
- 5 g fresh basil
- 1 teaspoon olive oil

Directions:
1. Cut the boneless chicken breast into medium pieces.
2. Mix the black pepper, paprika, turmeric, curry, and salt in a suitable mixing bowl and stir well.
3. Toss the cut-up chicken pieces with the spice mixture and coat well.
4. Chop the basil and mix it with the butter in a small bowl.
5. Stir the mixture until smooth. Set the temperature Ninja Foodi to" Sauté" mode.
6. Add the butter mixture into the Ninja Foodi. Melt it.
7. Transfer the chicken filets into the Ninja Foodi and sauté them for 10 min.
8. Add the olive oil and fish sauce.
9. Close the Ninja Foodi's lid and cook the dish on "Sear/Sauté" mode for 25 min.
10. Once cooked, remove the chicken from the Ninja Foodi.
11. Let the dish rest briefly and serve.

Nutrition Values Per Serving:
Calories: 182, Total fat: 12g, Fiber: 1g, Carbohydrates: 12.7g, Protein: 6g

Creamy Chicken Pancake

Prep Time: 20 min Cooking time: 15 min Servings: 9
Ingredients:

- 136 g flour
- 3 eggs
- 1 teaspoon salt
- 1 teaspoon psyllium husk powder
- 50 g half and half
- ½ tablespoon baking soda
- 1 tablespoon apple cider vinegar
- 1 medium onion
- ½ teaspoon black pepper
- 7 ounces ground chicken
- 1 teaspoon paprika
- 1 tablespoon tomato paste
- 1 tablespoon butter
- 1 tablespoon olive oil
- 1 tablespoon sour cream

Directions:

1. Beat the eggs in a suitable mixing bowl, add half and half and flour, and whisk until smooth batter forms.
2. Add the baking soda, salt, apple cider vinegar, and psyllium husk powder, and stir well.
3. Let the prepared batter rest for 10 min in the refrigerator.
4. Peel the onion and dice it. Mix the ground chicken with the black pepper, paprika, tomato paste, kosher salt, and sour cream in a suitable mixing bowl and stir well.
5. Set the temperature Ninja Foodi to" Sauté" mode. Add the ground chicken mixture and sauté the meat for 10 min, stirring frequently.
6. Remove the chicken from the Ninja Foodi. Pour the sesame oil and begin to cook the pancakes.
7. Ladle a small amount of the batter into the Ninja Foodi.
8. Cook the chicken pancakes for 1 minute per side.
9. Place one pancake into the Ninja Foodi and spread it with the ground chicken.
10. Repeat the step until you form a pancake cake.
11. Close the Ninja's lid and cook the dish on" Pressure" mode for 10 min.
12. Once cooked, remove the cake from the Ninja Foodi and let it rest briefly.
13. Cut into slices and serve.

Nutrition Values Per Serving:
Calories: 134, Total fat: 9.4g, Fiber: 1g, Carbohydrates: 3.4g, Protein: 9.6g

Sriracha Chicken Satay

Prep Time: 10 min Cooking time: 16 min Servings: 8
Ingredients:

- 10 ounces boneless chicken thighs
- 120 ml sweet soy sauce
- 120 ml dark soy sauce
- 1 teaspoon lemongrass paste
- 1 tablespoon almond oil
- 1 teaspoon salt
- 1 tablespoon scallions
- ½ tablespoon sriracha

Directions:
1. Chop the chicken thighs and sprinkle them with the lemongrass paste and salt and stir well.
2. Set the temperature Ninja Foodi to" Pressure" mode. Place the chicken thighs into the Ninja Foodi and add the soy sauces.
3. Chop the scallions and add them into the Ninja Foodi.
4. Top the mixture with the sriracha and almond oil, stir well using a spoon and Close the Ninja's lid.
5. Cook on "Pressure" mode for 16 min at high.
6. Once cooked, release the pressure and open the lid.
7. Transfer the cooked chicken satay to a serving plate and sprinkle it with the sauce from the Ninja Foodi.
8. Serve the dish hot.

Nutrition Values Per Serving:
Calories: 85, Total fat: 4.7g, Fiber: 0g, Carbohydrates: 1.98g, Protein: 9g

Saucy Chicken Breast

Prep Time: 15 min Cooking time: 40 min Servings: 8
Ingredients:

- 2 pounds of chicken breasts
- 2 tbsp ketchup
- 100 g   Sugar
- 85 g of soy sauce
- 1 teaspoon salt
- 2 ounces fresh rosemary
- 1 teaspoon ground white pepper
- 34 g garlic
- 2 tbsp olive oil
- 1 white onion
- 4 tbsp water
- 1 tablespoon flax meal
- ⅓ teaspoon red Chilli flakes
- 1 teaspoon oregano

Directions:
1. Place the chicken breast into the Ninja Foodi. Set the temperature Ninja Foodi to" Pressure" mode.
2. Mix the ketchup, sugar, soy sauce, salt, rosemary, and ground white pepper in a suitable mixing bowl and whisk until smooth.
3. Peel the garlic and white onion, and then slice the vegetables.
4. Mix the sliced vegetables with the chile flakes and oregano and stir.
5. Place Sugar mixture into the Ninja Foodi. Mix well, Close the Ninja's lid, and cook for 10 min.
6. Mix flax meal with water in a suitable mixing bowl.
7. Once it is done, release the cooker's pressure and open the lid.
8. Remove the chicken breast from the Ninja Foodi and chop it.
9. Pour the starch mixture into the Ninja Foodi and stir. Add the chicken and Close the Ninja's lid.
10. Cook the chicken on "Sauté" mode for 30 min.
11. Once it is done, remove the dish from the Ninja Foodi, let it rest briefly, and serve.

Nutrition Values Per Serving:
Calories: 295, Total fat: 13.4g, Fiber: 3.9g, Carbohydrates: 9.5g, Protein: 34.6g

Chicken Cheese Bowl

Prep Time: 15 min Cooking time: 30 min Servings: 6
Ingredients:

- 7 ounces Feta cheese
- 10 ounces boneless chicken breast
- 1 teaspoon basil
- 1 tablespoon onion powder
- 1 teaspoon olive oil
- 1 tablespoon sesame oil
- 4 ounces green olives
- 2 cucumbers
- 237 ml of water
- 1 teaspoon salt

Directions:
1. Set the temperature Ninja Foodi to" Pressure" mode.

2. Place the boneless chicken breast into the Ninja Foodi.
3. Add water, basil, and onion powder, stir well and Close the Ninja's lid.
4. Cook on "Pressure" mode at High for 30 min.
5. Chop the Feta cheese roughly and sprinkle it with olive oil.
6. Slice the green olives. Chop the cucumbers into medium-sized cubes.
7. Mix the chopped cheese, sliced green olives, and cucumbers in a suitable mixing bowl.
8. Top the mixture with salt and sesame oil.
9. When the chicken is cooked, open the Ninja Foodi and remove it from the machine.
10. Allow the chicken to cool a little and chop roughly.
11. Return this chicken to the cheese mixture.
12. Mix well and serve.

Nutrition Values Per Serving:
Calories: 279, Total fat: 19.8g, Fiber: 2g, Carbohydrates: 15.37g, Protein: 11g

Duck Meat Tacos

Prep Time: 10 min Cooking time: 22 min Servings: 7
Ingredients:

- 1-pound duck breast fillet
- 1 teaspoon salt
- 1 teaspoon Chilli powder
- 1 teaspoon onion powder
- 1 teaspoon oregano
- 1 teaspoon basil
- 75 g lettuce
- 1 teaspoon black pepper
- 1 tablespoon tomato sauce
- 200 ml chicken stock
- 1 tablespoon olive oil
- 6 ounces Cheddar cheese
- 7 flour tortilla
- 1 teaspoon turmeric

Directions:
1. Chop the duck fillet and transfer it to the blender.
2. Blend the mixture well. Set the temperature Ninja Foodi to" Sauté" mode.
3. Place the blended duck fillet into the Ninja Foodi.
4. Sprinkle it with olive oil and stir well. Sauté the dish for 5 min.
5. Mix the salt, Chilli powder, onion powder, oregano, basil, black pepper, and turmeric in a suitable mixing bowl and stir.
6. Add tomato sauce. Sprinkle the blended duck fillet with the spice mixture.
7. Mix well and add chicken stock. Stir gently and Close the Ninja's lid.
8. Cook the mixture at the" Pressure" mode for 17 min.
9. Wash the lettuce and chop it roughly. Grate the Cheddar cheese.
10. When the duck mixture is cooked, remove it from the Ninja Foodi and let it rest briefly.
11. Place the chopped lettuce in the tortillas.
12. Add the duck mixture to tortillas and top it with sliced in grater cheese.
13. Serve.

Nutrition Values Per Serving:
Calories: 246, Total fat: 12.9g, Fiber: 1.6g, Carbohydrates: 4.1g, Protein: 28.9g

Salsa Verde Dipped Chicken

Prep Time: 10 min Cooking time: 30 min Servings: 6
Ingredients:

- 10 ounces Salsa Verde
- 1 tablespoon paprika
- 1-pound boneless chicken breasts
- 1 teaspoon salt
- 1 teaspoon ground coriander
- 1 teaspoon cilantro

Directions:

1. Rub the boneless chicken breasts with paprika, salt, black pepper, and cilantro. Set the temperature Ninja Foodi to" Pressure" mode.
2. Place the boneless chicken into the Ninja Foodi.
3. Sprinkle the meat with the salsa Verde and stir well.
4. Close the Ninja Foodi's lid and cook for 30 min.
5. Once it is done, release the pressure and transfer the chicken to the mixing bowl.
6. Shred the chicken well and serve.

Nutrition Values Per Serving:
Calories: 222, Total fat: 11.3g, Fiber: 3g, Carbohydrates: 21.02g, Protein: 9g

Onions Stuffed with Chicken

Prep Time: 15 min Cooking time: 40 min Servings: 5
Ingredients:

- 5 large white onions, chopped
- 1-pound ground chicken
- 231 g cream
- 200 ml chicken stock
- 1 teaspoon salt
- 1 teaspoon oregano
- 1 teaspoon basil
- 1 egg
- 1 teaspoon turmeric
- 5 garlic cloves

Directions:

1. Place the ground chicken in a suitable mixing bowl and sprinkle it with salt, oregano, basil, and turmeric.
2. Stir in egg and mix well evenly.
3. Set the temperature Ninja Foodi to" Sear/Sauté" mode. Transfer the stuffed onions to the Ninja Foodi.
4. Add the chicken stock and cream. Close the Ninja's lid and cook for 40 min.
5. Once it is done, open the lid and let the onions sit for 2 min.
6. Transfer the stuffed onions to a serving plate and sprinkle them with the liquid from the Ninja Foodi.
7. Serve warm.

Nutrition Values Per Serving:
Calories: 318, Total fat: 19.3g, Fiber: 2g, Carbohydrates: 15.56g, Protein: 22g

Chicken Cutlets

Prep Time: 10 min Cooking time: 25 min Servings: 8
Ingredients:

- 14 ounces ground chicken
- 1 teaspoon black pepper
- 1 teaspoon paprika
- 1 teaspoon cilantro
- 1 teaspoon oregano
- ½ teaspoon minced garlic
- 2 tbsp starch
- 1 teaspoon red chile flakes
- 1 tablespoon oatmeal flour
- 1 egg

Directions:

1. Place the ground chicken in a suitable mixing bowl.
2. Sprinkle it with black pepper, cilantro, and oregano.
3. Add paprika and minced garlic and mix using your hands.
4. Beat the egg in a separate bowl.
5. Add the starch and oatmeal flour to the egg and stir well until smooth.
6. Add the egg mixture to the ground meat.
7. Add the Chilli flakes and mix well. Make the medium cutlets from the ground chicken mixture.
8. Set the temperature Ninja Foodi to" Steam" mode.
9. Transfer the chicken cutlets to the Ninja Foodi trivet and place the trivet into the Ninja Foodi.
10. Close the Ninja's lid and cook the chicken cutlets on Steam mode for 25 min.
11. Once cooked, remove the food from the Ninja Foodi, let it rest, and serve.

Nutrition Values Per Serving:
Calories: 96, Total fat: 5.3g, Fiber: 0g, Carbohydrates: 1.89g, Protein: 10g

Savory Pulled Chicken

Prep Time: 10 min Cooking time: 22 min Servings: 7
Ingredients

- 1-pound chicken breast, boneless
- 1 tablespoon Sugar
- 1 teaspoon black pepper
- 1 teaspoon olive oil
- 473 ml of water
- 1 ounce's bay leaf
- 1 tablespoon basil
- 1 tablespoon butter
- 120 g cream
- 1 teaspoon salt
- 3 garlic cloves
- 1 teaspoon turmeric

Directions:

1. Set the temperature Ninja Foodi to" Pressure" mode.
2. Pour water into the Ninja Foodi and add the chicken breast.
3. Add the bay leaf. Close the Ninja's lid and cook for 12 min.
4. Once it is done, release the cooker's pressure and open the Ninja Foodi's lid.

5. Transfer the chicken breast to a mixing bowl and shred it.
6. Sprinkle the shredded chicken with sugar, black pepper, basil, butter, cream, salt, and turmeric and stir well.
7. Peel the garlic cloves and mince them.
8. Spray the Ninja Foodi with the olive oil inside and transfer the shredded chicken into a Ninja Foodi.
9. Cook the dish on" Sauté" mode for 10 min.
10. Once cooked, transfer it to a serving plate.
11. Devour

Nutrition Values Per Serving:
Calories: 122, Total fat: 5.3g, Fiber: 1.3g, Carbohydrates: 4.4g, Protein: 14.4g

Chicken with Pomegranate Sauce

Prep Time: 10 min Cooking time: 29 min Servings: 6
Ingredients:
- 118 ml pomegranate juice
- 2 tbsp Sugar
- 1 teaspoon cinnamon
- 60 ml chicken stock
- 2 pounds of chicken breast
- 1 teaspoon starch
- 1 teaspoon butter
- 1 tablespoon oregano
- 1 teaspoon turmeric
- ½ teaspoon red chili flakes

Directions:
1. Set the temperature Ninja Foodi to" Pressure" mode. Put the chicken breast into the Ninja Foodi and sprinkle it with oregano, butter, chicken stock, and chile flakes.
2. Stir the mixture and close the Ninja Foodi's lid. Cook the meat for 20 min.
3. Mix the pomegranate juice, sugar, cinnamon, starch, and turmeric and stir well until everything is dissolved.
4. Once it is done, open the Ninja Foodi's lid and remove the chicken.
5. Set the temperature Ninja Foodi to" Sauté" mode.
6. Pour the pomegranate sauce into the Ninja Foodi and sauté it for 4 min.
7. Return the chicken back into the Ninja Foodi and stir the dish using a spoon.
8. Close the Ninja's lid and cook the chicken in" Pressure" mode for 5 min.
9. Once it is done, release the cooker's pressure then remove the Ninja Foodi's lid.
10. Transfer the juicy chicken to a serving plate.
11. Drizzle the pomegranate sauce on top.

Nutrition Values Per Serving:
Calories: 198, Total fat: 4.6g, Fiber: 0.6g, Carbohydrates: 4.7g, Protein: 32.2g

Baked Parmesan Chicken

Prep Time: 10 min Cooking time: 30 min Servings: 8
Ingredients:
- 200 g chopped tomato
- 3 tbsp butter
- 1-pound boneless chicken breast

- 1 teaspoon salt
- 1 teaspoon paprika
- 7 ounces Parmesan cheese
- 10 g fresh basil
- 1 teaspoon cilantro
- 1 tablespoon sour cream

Directions:
1. Grate the Parmesan cheese, mix it with the cilantro and paprika in a suitable mixing bowl, and stir.
2. Sprinkle the boneless chicken breast with the salt and place it into the Ninja Foodi.
3. Add the basil, butter, tomato, and sour cream.
4. Sprinkle the chicken with the sliced in grater cheese mixture and Close the Ninja's lid.
5. Cook the chicken on "Pressure" mode for 30 min at High.
6. Once it is done, release the cooker's pressure then remove the Ninja Foodi's lid.
7. Transfer the dish to a serving plate.

Nutrition Values Per Serving:
Calories: 234, Total fat: 14.2g, Fiber: 0.4g, Carbohydrates: 2g, Protein: 24.8g

Seasoned Chicken Strips

Prep Time: 10 min Cooking time: 8 min Servings: 7
Ingredients:
- 120 g flour
- 1 teaspoon kosher salt
- 1 teaspoon cayenne pepper
- ½ teaspoon cilantro
- ½ teaspoon oregano
- ½ teaspoon paprika
- 125 ml of coconut milk
- 1-pound chicken fillet
- 3 tbsp sesame oil
- 1 teaspoon turmeric

Directions:
1. Place the flour in a suitable mixing bowl.
2. Add kosher salt, cayenne pepper, cilantro, oregano, paprika, and turmeric and mix well.
3. Pour the coconut milk into a separate bowl. Cut the chicken into strips.
4. Set the temperature Ninja Foodi to" Sauté" mode. Pour the olive oil into the Ninja Foodi.
5. Dip the chicken strips in the coconut milk, then dip them in the flour mixture.
6. Repeat this step two more times.
7. Add the dipped chicken strips to the Ninja Foodi.
8. Sauté the chicken strips for 3 min on each side.
9. Transfer the chicken to a paper towel to drain any excess oil before serving.
10. Serve warm.

Nutrition Values Per Serving:
Calories: 244, Total fat: 18.1g, Fiber: 1.6g, Carbohydrates: 10.6g, Protein: 11.9g

Herbed Chicken Wings

Prep Time: 10 min Cooking time: 20 min Servings: 7
Ingredients:

- 4 tbsp dry dill
- 285 g Greek yogurt
- 1 teaspoon salt
- 1 teaspoon black pepper
- ½ teaspoon red chile flakes
- 1 teaspoon oregano
- 1 tablespoon olive oil
- 1-pound chicken wings
- 1 teaspoon lemon juice

Directions:

1. Mix the yogurt, salt, black pepper, Chilli flakes, oregano, and lemon juice in a suitable mixing bowl, blending until smooth.
2. Add 2 tbsp dill and stir well. Add the chicken wings and coat them with the yogurt mixture.
3. Let the chicken wings rest for 2 hours.
4. Set the temperature Ninja Foodi to "Pressure" mode. Pour the olive oil into the Ninja Foodi.
5. Add the chicken wings. Sprinkle the chicken wings with the remaining dill.
6. Close the Ninja Foodi and cook for 20 min.
7. Once the wings are cooked, then remove them from the Ninja Foodi.
8. Let the wings rest briefly and serve.

Nutrition Values Per Serving:
Calories: 122, Total fat: 4.5g, Fiber: 1g, Carbohydrates: 2.77g, Protein: 17g

Cheesy Chicken Fillets

Prep Time: 10 min Cooking time: 15 min Servings: 7
Ingredients:

- 231 g cream cheese
- 6 ounces Cheddar cheese
- 1 yellow onion
- 14 ounces boneless chicken breast
- 1 teaspoon olive oil
- 1 tablespoon black pepper
- 1 teaspoon red chile flakes
- 4 ounces apricot, pitted
- 3 tbsp chicken stock

Directions:

1. Cut the chicken breast into fillets and sprinkle the boneless chicken breasts with the black pepper, olive oil, and chile flakes.
2. Set the temperature Ninja Foodi to" Sauté" mode. Transfer the chicken breasts into the Ninja Foodi and sauté for 5 min per side.
3. Meanwhile, grate the Cheddar cheese and mix it with the cream cheese.
4. Add chicken stock and mix well using a spoon.
5. Mix apricots with sliced onions in a bowl.
6. Once it is done, open the Ninja Foodi's lid.
7. Sprinkle the chicken with the onion mixture.
8. Add the Cheddar cheese mixture.
9. close the Ninja's lid and cook at the" Pressure" mode for 10 min.
10. Once it is done, release the cooker's pressure and open the Ninja Foodi's lid.
11. Transfer the chicken to the serving plates.

Nutrition Values Per Serving:
Calories: 282, Total fat: 18.1g, Fiber: 1g, Carbohydrates: 11.88g, Protein: 18g

BBQ Chicken Meatballs

Prep Time: 10 min Cooking time: 25 min Servings: 8
Ingredients:

- 280 g BBQ sauce
- 1 teaspoon salt
- 1 teaspoon sugar
- 3 tbsp chives
- 12 ounces ground chicken
- 1 egg
- 1 tablespoon coconut flour
- 1 tablespoon olive oil
- 1 teaspoon oregano
- 1 red onion

Directions:

1. Put the ground chicken in a suitable mixing bowl.
2. Sprinkle the ground meat with sugar, salt, chives, coconut flour, and oregano.
3. Peel the red onion, dice it, and add the onion to the ground chicken mixture.
4. Beat the egg in a suitable bowl and add it to the ground chicken.
5. Mix everything well using your hands until smooth.
6. Make small balls from the ground chicken.
7. Set the temperature Ninja Foodi to" Sauté" mode. Pour the olive oil into the Ninja Foodi.
8. Put the chicken balls in the Ninja Foodi and sauté them for 5 min.
9. Stir them constantly to make all the sides of the chicken balls are brown.
10. Pour the barbecue sauce into the Ninja Foodi and Close the Ninja's lid.
11. Cook the dish on "Sear/Sauté" mode for 20 min.
12. Once it is done, remove the dish from the Ninja Foodi and serve.

Nutrition Values Per Serving:
Calories: 131, Total fat: 5.7g, Fiber: 0.8g, Carbohydrates: 6.3g, Protein: 13.3g

Chicken Dumplings

Prep Time: 10 min Cooking time: 25 min Servings: 7
Ingredients:

- 1 teaspoon salt
- ¼ teaspoon Sugar
- 120 g flour
- ¼ cup whey
- 10 oz boneless chicken breast
- 1 tablespoon olive oil
- 237 ml of water
- 1 onion
- 1 teaspoon black pepper
- 1 teaspoon paprika

Directions:

1. Mix salt, sugar, and flour in a suitable mixing bowl and stir.
2. Add the whey and mix well. Knead the dough.
3. Make a long log from the dough and cut it into small dumpling pieces.
4. Chop the chicken roughly and sprinkle it with the black pepper.
5. Place the chopped chicken into the Ninja Foodi.

6. Set the temperature Ninja Foodi to" Pressure" mode.
7. Sprinkle the chopped chicken with olive oil and add water.
8. Close the Ninja Foodi's lid and cook for 15 min. Peel the onion and slice it.
9. Once it is done, release the cooker's pressure and open the Ninja Foodi's lid.
10. Remove the cooked chicken and shred it. Return the chicken back to the Ninja Foodi.
11. Add the dumplings and sliced onion. Sprinkle the dish with paprika.
12. Close the Ninja Foodi's lid and cook the dish on" Pressure" mode for 10 min.
13. Once it is done, remove the dish from the Ninja Foodi, let it rest briefly, and serve.

Nutrition Values Per Serving:
Calories: 133, Total fat: 7.1g, Fiber: 1g, Carbohydrates: 4.5g, Protein: 13.1g

Chicken Rissoles

Prep Time: 10 min Cooking time: 15 min Servings: 8
Ingredients:

- 4 egg yolks
- 1 tablespoon turmeric
- 1 teaspoon salt
- 1 teaspoon dried parsley
- 1 tablespoon cream
- 12 ounces ground chicken
- 1 tablespoon almond oil
- 1 tablespoon sesame seeds
- 1 teaspoon minced garlic

Directions:
1. Mix the turmeric, salt, dried parsley, and sesame seeds in a suitable mixing bowl.
2. Beat egg yolks in a mini bowl and pour in to the ground chicken in a large bowl.
3. Add the spice mixture and garlic and combine.
4. Make small rissoles from the ground chicken mixture. Set the temperature Ninja Foodi to" Sauté" mode.
5. Pour the olive oil into the Ninja Foodi and add the chicken rissoles.
6. Sauté the chicken rissoles for 15 min, stirring frequently.
7. Once cooked, serve.

Nutrition Values Per Serving:
Calories: 117, Total fat: 8.4g, Fiber: 0g, Carbohydrates: 1.42g, Protein: 9g

Chicken Broth with Fresh Herbs

Prep Time: 10 min Cooking time: 45 min Servings: 13
Ingredients:

- 8 ounces drumsticks
- 8 ounces of chicken wings
- 14 g fresh thyme
- 2.25 g cup fresh dill
- 6 g fresh parsley
- 1 teaspoon black pepper
- 2365 ml of water
- 1 teaspoon salt
- 2 tbsp fresh rosemary

- 1 garlic clove
- 1 onion

Directions:
1. Wash the drumsticks and chicken wings carefully.
2. Chop them roughly and transfer the ingredients to the Ninja Foodi.
3. Set the temperature Ninja Foodi to" Sauté" mode. Top the mixture with the salt and black pepper and stir well using your hands.
4. Wash the thyme, dill, and parsley and chop them. Put the chopped greens into the Ninja Foodi.
5. Add water and rosemary. Peel the onion and garlic.
6. Add the vegetables to the chicken mixture.
7. Close the Ninja Foodi's lid and cook the dish for 45 min.
8. Once it is done, discard the greens from the Ninja Foodi.
9. Remove the chicken from the Ninja Foodi.
10. Strain the chicken stock and serve it with the cooked chicken.
11. Serve warm.

Nutrition Values Per Serving:
Calories: 35, Total fat: 0.7g, Fiber: 1g, Carbohydrates: 3.06g, Protein: 4g

Peanut Butter Duck

Prep Time: 10 min Cooking time: 25 min Servings: 6
Ingredients:
- 4 tbsp creamy peanut butter
- 5 g fresh dill
- 1 teaspoon oregano
- 1 tablespoon lemon juice
- 1 teaspoon lime zest
- ¼ teaspoon cinnamon
- 1 teaspoon turmeric
- 1 teaspoon paprika
- ½ teaspoon cumin
- ½ teaspoon black pepper
- 200 ml chicken stock
- 1 tablespoon butter
- 1-pound duck breast
- 60 ml red wine

Directions:
1. Mix the chopped dill with the lime zest, cinnamon, turmeric, lemon juice, paprika, cumin, and black pepper and stir well.
2. Set the temperature Ninja Foodi to" Pressure" mode.
3. Rub the duck with the spice mixture and place it into the Ninja Foodi.
4. Sprinkle the meat with oregano. Add the chicken stock, red wine, and butter.
5. Close the Ninja Foodi's lid and cook on "Pressure" mode for 18 min at High.
6. Once it is done, release the cooker's pressure then remove the Ninja Foodi's lid.
7. Set the temperature Ninja Foodi to" Sauté" mode. Remove the dish from the Ninja Foodi.
8. Add the peanut butter into the Ninja Foodi and sauté it for 1 minute.
9. Add the duck and sauté the dish for 5 min.
10. Stir the duck a couple of times.
11. Once done, transfer the duck to a serving plate and let it rest briefly before serving.

Nutrition Values Per Serving:
Calories: 198, Total fat: 11.5g, Fiber: 1g, Carbohydrates: 4.74g, Protein: 19g

Creamy Chicken Dip

Prep Time: 15 min Cooking time: 30 min Servings: 8
Ingredients:

- 2 tbsp miso paste
- 1 teaspoon liquid stevia
- 1 teaspoon apple cider vinegar
- 60 g cream
- ½ teaspoon white pepper
- 3 tbsp chicken stock
- 7 ounces boneless chicken breast
- 1 teaspoon black-eyed peas
- 708 ml of water

Directions:
1. Chop the chicken breast roughly and place it into the Ninja Foodi.
2. Set the temperature Ninja Foodi to "Sear/Sauté" mode. Add water, black-eyed peas, and white pepper.
3. Stir the mixture and Close the Ninja's lid. Cook the dish on poultry mode for 30 min.
4. Mix the miso paste and chicken stock in a suitable mixing bowl.
5. Add liquid stevia and apple cider vinegar.
6. Whisk the mixture carefully until miso paste is dissolved.
7. When the chicken is cooked, remove it from the Ninja Foodi and let it rest briefly.
8. Transfer the chicken to a blender and add cream.
9. Blend the mixture for 5 min or until smooth.
10. Add the miso paste mixture and blend the mixture for 1 minute.
11. Transfer the cooked chicken dip to a serving dish and serve.

Nutrition Values Per Serving:
Calories: 62, Total fat: 2.5g, Fiber: 0.3g, Carbohydrates: 1.6g, Protein: 7.8g

Crispy Duck Cutlets

Prep Time: 10 min Cooking time: 20 min Servings: 8
Ingredients:

- 65 ml vermouth
- 1-pound ground duck
- 1 teaspoon salt
- 4 ounces keto bread
- 60 g cream
- 1 teaspoon paprika
- 1 teaspoon coconut flour
- 1 teaspoon white pepper

Directions:
1. Mix the ground duck and vermouth in a suitable mixing bowl.
2. Chop the bread and mix it with the cream and stir well until smooth.
3. Use a blender, if necessary. Add the bread mixture to the ground duck.
4. Sprinkle the meat mixture with salt, paprika, and white pepper.
5. Add coconut flour and mix well using a spoon.
6. Make the medium cutlets from the duck mixture and transfer them to the trivet.
7. Set the temperature Ninja Foodi to" Steam" mode.
8. Place the Ninja's trivet into the Ninja Foodi and Close the Ninja's lid.

9. Cook the dish on steam mode for 20 min.
10. Once it is done, remove the cutlets from the Ninja Foodi. Rest briefly and serve.

Nutrition Values Per Serving:
Calories: 121, Total fat: 5.4g, Fiber: 1.4g, Carbohydrates: 4.9g, Protein: 12.3g

Creamy Chicken Soup

Prep Time: 15 min Cooking time: 22 min Servings: 8
Ingredients:

- 946 ml of water
- 500 ml cream
- 43 g half and half
- 1 tablespoon minced garlic
- 5 ounces mushrooms, chopped
- 1 onion
- 1 tablespoon olive oil
- ½ tablespoon salt
- 1 teaspoon fresh basil
- 1 teaspoon fresh dill
- 7 ounces chicken breast

Directions:
1. Peel the onion. Set the temperature Ninja Foodi to" Sauté" mode.
2. Transfer the onion and mushroom to the Ninja Foodi and add olive oil.
3. Sauté the vegetable mixture for 5 min, stirring constantly.
4. Add chicken and cream. Add the half and half and water.
5. Top the mixture with garlic, salt, dill, and basil, stir well, and Close the Ninja's lid.
6. Cook the dish for 20 min in the" Pressure" mode.
7. Open the Ninja Foodi's lid and remove the chicken breast and shred it.
8. Blend the soup mixture using an immersion blender until smooth.
9. Add the shredded chicken and close the Ninja Foodi's lid.
10. Cook the soup at the" Pressure" mode for 2 min.
11. Ladle the cooked soup into serving bowls.

Nutrition Values Per Serving:
Calories: 106, Total fat: 6.9g, Fiber: 0.5g, Carbohydrates: 4.6g, Protein: 6.9g

Spicy Pulled Duck

Prep Time: 10 min Cooking time: 27 min Servings: 8
Ingredients:

- 80 ml red wine
- 48 g chicken stock
- 1 teaspoon onion powder
- 14 ounces duck fillet
- 2 teaspoon cayenne pepper
- ¼ teaspoon minced garlic
- 3 g fresh dill
- 1 teaspoon salt
- 1 teaspoon black pepper
- 1 tablespoon sour cream

- 1 tablespoon tomato puree

Directions:
1. Mix the red wine and chicken stock in a suitable mixing bowl and stir.
2. Set the temperature Ninja Foodi to" Sauté" mode.
3. Pour the chicken stock mixture into the Ninja Foodi and preheat it for 1 minute.
4. Mix the onion powder, cayenne pepper, salt, black pepper, and garlic in a suitable mixing bowl.
5. Stir the mixture and sprinkle the duck fillet with the spice mixture.
6. Place the duck fillet into the Ninja Foodi and Close the Ninja's lid.
7. Cook the duck on" Pressure" mode for 25 min at High.
8. Once it is done, remove the dish from the Ninja Foodi and let it rest briefly.
9. Shred the duck using a fork. Leave a third of the liquid into the Ninja Foodi and return the shredded duck.
10. Add the tomato puree and sour cream. Chop the dill and sprinkle the dish with it.
11. Stir it gently and Close the Ninja's lid.
12. Cook the dish on" Sauté" mode for 2 min.
13. Once it is done, transfer the hot dish to a serving plate and serve.

Nutrition Values Per Serving:
Calories: 119, Total fat: 7.9g, Fiber: 0g, Carbohydrates: 1.81g, Protein: 9g

Oregano Chicken Drumsticks

Prep Time: 5 min Cooking time: 18 min Servings: 7
Ingredients:
- 1-pound chicken drumsticks
- 1 teaspoon salt
- 1 teaspoon paprika
- 1 teaspoon white pepper
- 237 ml of water
- 1 teaspoon thyme
- ½ teaspoon oregano

Directions:
1. Sprinkle the chicken drumsticks with salt, paprika, thyme, oregano, and white pepper and stir well.
2. Set the temperature Ninja Foodi to" Pressure" mode at High.
3. Place the chicken drumsticks into the Ninja Foodi and add the water.
4. Close the Ninja's lid and cook for 18 min.
5. Once it is done, release the cooker's pressure and open the Ninja Foodi's lid.
6. Remove the drumsticks from the Ninja Foodi and transfer them to the serving platter.

Nutrition Values Per Serving:
Calories: 112, Total fat: 3.8g, Fiber: 0g, Carbohydrates: 0.5g, Protein: 17.9g

Creamy Chicken Stew

Prep Time: 15 min Cooking time: 35 min Servings: 8
Ingredients
- 121 g cup tomato juice
- 1 tablespoon sugar
- 1 teaspoon salt
- 1-pound boneless chicken breast
- 1 tablespoon oregano

- 1 teaspoon cilantro
- 1 teaspoon fresh ginger, peeled and chopped
- 2 carrots, peeled and chopped
- 3 red onion, peeled and chopped
- 5 ounces shallot, chopped
- 1 tablespoon black pepper
- 120 g cream
- 710 ml chicken stock
- 3 ounces scallions, chopped
- 2 tbsp olive oil
- 3 ounces eggplants, peeled and chopped

Directions:
1. Mix the tomato juice with the oregano, salt, black pepper, cilantro, and cream in a suitable mixing bowl and stir.
2. Set the temperature Ninja Foodi to" Sauté" mode.
3. Add chopped vegetables to the Ninja Foodi and drizzle olive oil.
4. Sauté these vegetables for 5 min.
5. Add the tomato juice mixture and the rest of the ingredients to the pot.
6. Stir well using a spoon and close the Ninja Foodi's lid.
7. Cook chicken on" Pressure" mode for 30 min.
8. Release the pressure naturally, then remove the lid.
9. Serve warm.

Nutrition Values Per Serving:
Calories: 205, Total fat: 9g, Fiber: 2.5g, Carbohydrates: 13.7g, Protein: 18.4g

Baked Chicken Bread

Prep Time: 15 min Cooking time: 40 min Servings: 8
Ingredients:
- ½ tablespoon garam masala powder
- 8 ounces keto dough
- 1 teaspoon sesame seeds
- 1 egg yolk
- 1 teaspoon ground cilantro
- 1 teaspoon dill
- 10 ounces ground chicken
- 6 g fresh parsley
- 1 teaspoon olive oil
- 1 tablespoon black pepper
- 1 onion

Directions:
1. Roll the dough using a rolling pin. Mix the ground chicken with the ground cilantro and black pepper and stir well.
2. Wash the parsley carefully and chop it. Add the parsley to the chicken mixture.
3. Peel the onion and dice it. Add the onion to the chicken mixture.
4. Mix the meat mixture using your hands. Set the temperature Ninja Foodi to" Pressure" mode.
5. Place the ground meat mixture in the middle of the rolled dough.
6. Wrap the dough in the shape of the bread.
7. Spray the Ninja Foodi with the olive oil inside and put the chicken bread there.
8. Whisk the egg yolk and sprinkle the chicken bread with it.
9. Sprinkle the dish with sesame seeds.

10. Close the Ninja Foodi's lid and cook the dish for 40 min.
11. Once it is done, open the Ninja Foodi's lid and check to see if the dish is cooked using a toothpick.
12. Transfer the chicken bread to a serving plate and let it rest briefly.
13. Slice it and serve.

Nutrition Values Per Serving:
Calories: 189, Total fat: 5.3g, Fiber: 4.2g, Carbohydrates: 8.1g, Protein: 27.3g

---

Zesty Duck Legs

Prep Time: 10 min Cooking time: 25min Servings: 6
Ingredients:

- 1-pound duck legs
- 118 ml pomegranate juice
- 4.5 g dill
- 1 teaspoon salt
- 1 teaspoon black pepper
- 1 teaspoon ground ginger
- 1 tablespoon olive oil
- 120 ml of water
- 1 teaspoon brown sugar
- 1 tablespoon lime zest
- 2 teaspoon soy sauce
- ⅓ teaspoon peppercorn

Directions:
1. Mix the black pepper, salt, lime zest, ground ginger, brown sugar, and peppercorn in a suitable mixing bowl and stir well.
2. Sprinkle the duck legs with the spice mixture and mix well using your hands.
3. Add the soy sauce, water, olive oil, and pomegranate juice.
4. Wash the dill and chop it. Sprinkle the duck legs mixture with the chopped dill.
5. Set the temperature Ninja Foodi to" Pressure" mode at High.
6. Transfer the duck legs mixture into the Ninja Foodi and Close the Ninja's lid.
7. Cook for 25 min. Once cooked, open the Ninja Foodi's lid and transfer the cooked duck legs to a serving dish.
8. Sprinkle the dish with the pomegranate sauce, if desired and serve

Nutrition Values Per Serving:
Calories: 209, Total fat: 11.4g, Fiber: 0g, Carbohydrates: 5.11g, Protein: 21g

---

Creamy Chicken Zoodles

Prep Time: 10 min Cooking time: 27 min Servings: 8
Ingredients:

- 5 ounces zoodles, cooked
- 1-pound boneless chicken breast
- 1 teaspoon cilantro
- 231 g cream
- 32 g chicken stock
- 1 teaspoon butter
- 1 teaspoon salt
- 120 g cream cheese

- 1 teaspoon paprika
- 1 teaspoon garlic powder

Directions:
1. Mix the cilantro, salt, paprika, and garlic powder in a suitable mixing bowl and stir well.
2. Sprinkle the boneless chicken breast with the spice mixture and mix well using your hands.
3. Set the temperature Ninja Foodi to" Pressure" mode. Place the spiced chicken into the Ninja Foodi.
4. Add cream, chicken stock, and cream cheese. Stir the mixture and close the Ninja Foodi's lid.
5. Cook the dish for 25 min. Open the lid and transfer the chicken to a mixing bowl.
6. Shred-it well using a fork. Transfer the shredded chicken into the Ninja Foodi.
7. Add cooked noodles, stir well, and Close the Ninja's lid.
8. Cook the zucchini noodles on" Pressure" mode for 2 min at High.
9. Remove the cooked dish from the Ninja Foodi. Serve it warm.

Nutrition Values Per Serving:
Calories: 186, Total fat: 18.9g, Fiber: 0.3g, Carbohydrates: 2.2g, Protein: 18g

Orange dipped Duck Breast

Prep Time: 10 min Cooking time: 37min Servings: 9
Ingredients:
- 2 pounds duck breast
- 2 oranges
- 2 tbsp honey
- 237 ml of water
- 1 teaspoon cayenne pepper
- 1 teaspoon salt
- 1 teaspoon curry powder
- 2 tbsp lemon juice
- 2 tbsp butter
- 1 teaspoon sugar
- 1 teaspoon turmeric

Directions:
1. Make the zest from the oranges and chop the fruits.
2. Mix the orange zest and chopped oranges in a suitable mixing bowl.
3. Top the mixture with the honey, cayenne pepper, salt, curry powder, lemon juice, sugar, and turmeric and stir well.
4. Set the temperature Ninja Foodi to" Sauté" mode. Put the duck in the orange mixture and stir it.
5. Add the butter into the Ninja Foodi and melt it at the sauté mode for 2 min.
6. Add water. Add the duck mixture and Close the Ninja's lid.
7. Set the temperature Ninja Foodi mode to "Poultry" and cook the dish for 35 min.
8. Once it is done, open the Ninja Foodi's lid and remove the duck from the Ninja Foodi.
9. Slice and transfer the duck to a serving plate.
10. Sprinkle the cooked dish with the orange sauce from the Ninja Foodi and serve.

Nutrition Values Per Serving:
Calories: 174, Total fat: 7g, Fiber: 1g, Carbohydrates: 7.18g, Protein: 20g

Chapter 5-Seafood and Fish Recipes

Seafood Stew

Prep Time: 10 min Cooking Time: 4 hours 50 min Servings: 8
Ingredients:
- 2 tbsp olive oil
- 1-pound tomatoes, chopped
- 1 large yellow onion, chopped finely
- 2 garlic cloves, minced
- 2 teaspoon curry powder
- 6 sprigs of fresh parsley
- Salt and black pepper, as required
- 1144 g chicken broth
- 1½ pounds salmon, cut into cubes
- 1½ pounds shrimp, peeled and deveined

Directions:
1. Into the Ninja Foodi's pot of Ninja Foodi, add all ingredients except seafood and mix well.
2. Close the Ninja Foodi with a crisping lid and select "Slow Cook". Set on "High" for 4 hours.
3. Hit the "Start/Stop" button to initiate cooking.
4. Once done, pen the Ninja's lid and stir in the seafood.
5. Now, set on "Pressure" mode at Low for 50 min.
6. Hit the "Start/Stop" button to initiate cooking.
7. Open the lid and serve hot.

Nutrition Values Per Serving:
Calories: 272, Total fat: 10.7g, Fiber: 1.1g, Carbohydrates: 6g, Protein: 38g

Buttered Salmon Fillets

Prep Time: 10 min Cooking Time: 10 min Servings: 2
Ingredients:
- 2 (6-ounce) salmon fillets
- Salt and black pepper, as required
- 1 tablespoon butter, melted

Directions:
1. Arrange the greased Air Fryer Basket into the Ninja Foodi's pot of Ninja Foodi.
2. Season salmon fillet with butter, salt and black pepper.
3. Arrange the salmon fillets into the prepared Air Fryer Basket in a single layer.
4. Close the Ninja Foodi with a crisping lid and select "Air Crisp" mode.
5. Set the temperature 360°F/ 183°C for almost 10 min.
6. Hit the "Start/Stop" button to initiate cooking.
7. Open the lid and serve hot.

Nutrition Values Per Serving:
Calories: 276, Total fat: 16.7g, Fiber: 0g, Carbohydrates: 12.06g, Protein: 33g

Creamy Salmon

Prep Time: 3 min Cooking Time: 10 min Servings: 2
Ingredients:

- 2 frozen salmon filets
- 118 ml of water
- 1 ½ teaspoon minced garlic
- 60 g heavy cream
- 1 cup parmesan cheese sliced in grater
- 1 tablespoon chopped fresh chives
- 1 tablespoon chopped fresh parsley
- 1 tablespoon fresh dill
- 1 teaspoon fresh lemon juice
- Salt and black pepper, to taste

Directions:

1. Add water and trivet to the pot. Place fillets on top of the trivet.
2. Close Ninja Foodi, press the pressure button, select high settings, and Set the temperature time to 4 min.
3. Once done cooking, do a quick release.
4. Transfer salmon to a serving plate. And remove trivet.
5. Press stop and then press the sauté button on Ninja Foodi.
6. Stir in heavy cream once the water begins to boil. Boil for 3 min.
7. Stir in lemon juice, parmesan cheese, dill, parsley, and chives.
8. Season with pepper and salt to taste
9. Serve and enjoy.

Nutrition Values Per Serving:
Calories: 423, Carbohydrates: 6.4g, Protein: 43.1g, Total fats 25.0g

Limed Haddock Fish

Prep Time: 15 min Cooking Time: 25 min Servings: 4
Ingredients:

- 1 garlic clove, minced
- ¼ teaspoon fresh ginger, sliced in grater finely
- 120 ml low-sodium soy sauce
- 57 g fresh lime juice
- 100 ml chicken broth
- 50 g of sugar
- ¼ teaspoon red pepper flakes, crushed
- 1-pound haddock steak

Directions:

1. Select "Sauté/Sear" mode of Ninja Foodi and place all ingredients except haddock steak.
2. Press "Start/Stop" to begin and cook for about 3-4 min, stirring continuously.
3. In a suitable bowl, reserve half of the marinade.
4. In a resealable bag, add the remaining marinade and haddock steak.
5. Seal the haddock's ziplock bag and shake it well to coat.
6. Refrigerate for about 30 min.
7. Arrange the greased Air Fryer Basket into the Ninja Foodi's pot of Ninja Foodi.
8. Close the Ninja Foodi with a crisping lid and select "Air Crisp" mode.
9. Set the temperature 390 °F/ 199 °C for almost 5 min.

10. Press "Start/Stop" to begin preheating.
11. After preheating, open the lid.
12. Place the haddock steak into the Air Fryer Basket.
13. Close the Ninja Foodi with a crisping lid and select "Air Crisp" mode.
14. Set the temperature 390 °F/ 199 °C for almost 11 min.
15. Hit the "Start/Stop" button to initiate cooking.
16. Open the lid and transfer the haddock steak onto a serving platter.
17. Immediately coat the haddock steaks with the remaining glaze.
18. Serve immediately.

Nutrition Values Per Serving:
Calories: 192, Total fat: 1.2g, Fiber: 1g, Carbohydrates: 15.1g, Protein: 3.2g

Basil Shrimp Scampi

Prep Time: 15 min Cooking Time: 7 min Servings: 3
Ingredients:

- 4 tbsp salted butter
- 1 tablespoon fresh lemon juice
- 1 tablespoon garlic, minced
- 2 teaspoon red pepper flakes, crushed
- 1-pound shrimp, peeled and deveined
- 2 tbsp fresh basil, chopped
- 1 tablespoon fresh chives, chopped
- 2 tbsp chicken broth

Directions:
1. Toss shrimp with the scampi ingredients in the Ninja Foodi's insert.
2. Close the Ninja Foodi with a crisping lid and select "Air Crisp" mode.
3. Set the temperature 325 °F/ 162 °C for almost 7 min.
4. Hit the "Start/Stop" button to initiate cooking.
5. Once done, open the lid and serve warm.

Nutrition Values Per Serving:
Calories: 245, Total fat: 16g, Fiber: 0.3g, Carbohydrates: 9g, Protein: 26g

Tuna Bake

Prep Time: 3 min Cooking Time: 10 min Servings: 2
Ingredients:

- 1 can cream-of-mushroom soup
- 354 ml water
- 150 g macaroni pasta
- 1 can tuna
- 72 g frozen peas
- ½ teaspoon salt
- 1 teaspoon pepper
- 117 g shredded cheddar cheese

Directions:
1. Mix soup and water in Ninja Foodi.
2. Add remaining ingredients except for cheese. Stir.
3. Close Ninja Foodi, press the pressure button, at high, and Set the temperature time to 4 min.

4. Once done cooking, do a quick release.
5. Remove the pressure lid.
6. Stir in cheese and roast for 5 min.
7. Serve and enjoy.

Nutrition Values Per Serving:

Calories: 378, Carbohydrates: 34.0g, Protein: 28.0g, Total fats 14.1g

Butter Dipped Crab Legs

Prep Time: 15 min Cooking Time: 4 min Servings: 2
Ingredients:

- 1½ pounds frozen crab legs
- Salt, as required
- 2 tbsp butter, melted

Directions:
1. Into the Ninja Foodi's pot of Ninja Foodi, place 237 ml of water and 1 teaspoon of salt.
2. Arrange the "Reversible Rack" into the Ninja Foodi's pot of Ninja Foodi.
3. Place the crab legs over the "Reversible Rack "and sprinkle with salt.
4. Close the Ninja Foodi's pressure lid.
5. Select "Pressure" and set it to "High" for 4 min.
6. Hit the "Start/Stop" button to initiate cooking.
7. Once done, quick release the cooker's pressure.
8. Open the lid and transfer crab legs onto a serving platter.
9. Drizzle with butter and serve.

Nutrition Values Per Serving:

Calories: 445, Total fat: 17g, Fiber: 0g, Carbohydrates: 0g, Protein: 65g

Salmon Bake

Prep Time: 5 min Cooking Time: 20 min Servings: 2
Ingredients:
- 96 g chicken broth
- 237 ml milk
- 1 salmon filet
- 2 tbsp olive oil
- Ground pepper to taste
- 1 teaspoon minced garlic
- 150 g of frozen vegetables
- ½ can of cream of celery soup
- ¼ teaspoon dill
- ¼ teaspoon cilantro
- 1 teaspoon Italian spice
- 1 teaspoon poultry seasoning
- 1 tablespoon ground parmesan

Directions:

1. Press the sauté button on Ninja Foodi and add oil to heat.
2. Place the salmon in the heated oil and cook for 2 min per side.
3. Stir in garlic, cook for 30 seconds then add broth and cook for 3 min.
4. Add the spices, milk, vegetables, noodles and stir.
5. Add the cream of celery soup on top and stir well.
6. Cover the pressure lid. Press the pressure cook button, select high settings and cook for 8 min.
7. Once done cooking, do a quick release.
8. Serve and enjoy with a sprinkle of parmesan.

Nutrition Values Per Serving:
Calories: 616, Carbohydrates: 28.7g, Protein: 51.8g, Total fats 32.6g

New Orleans Seafood Gumbo

Prep Time: 5 min Cooking Time: 20 min Servings: 2

Ingredients:

- 1 sea bass filet patted dry and cut into 2" chunks
- 1 tablespoon ghee or avocado oil
- 1 tablespoon Cajun seasoning
- 1 small yellow onion diced
- 1 small bell pepper diced
- 1 celery rib diced
- 2 Roma tomatoes diced
- 1 tablespoon tomato paste
- 1 bay leaf
- 237 mL bone broth
- ¾-pound medium to large raw shrimp deveined
- Sea salt
- Black pepper

Directions:

1. Press the sauté button and heat the oil.
2. Season fish chunks with pepper, salt, and half of Cajun seasoning.
3. When the oil is hot, sear fish chunks for 3 min per side and transfer to a plate.
4. Stir in remaining Cajun seasoning, celery, and onions. Sauté for 2 min.
5. Stir in bone broth, bay leaves, tomato paste, and diced tomatoes. Mix well. Add back fish.
6. Close Ninja Foodi, press the pressure cook button, select high settings, and Set the temperature time to 5 min.
7. Once done cooking, do a quick release.
8. Stir in shrimps, cover and cook 5 min in the residual heat.
9. Serve and enjoy.

Nutrition Values Per Serving:
Calories: 357, Carbohydrates: 14.8g, Protein: 45.9g, Total fats 12.6g

Tomato Dipped Tilapia

Prep Time: 2 min Cooking Time: 4 min Servings: 2

Ingredients:

- 2 tilapia fillets
- Salt and black pepper
- 2 Roma tomatoes, diced
- 2 minced garlic cloves
- 20 g chopped basil, fresh
- 1 tablespoon olive oil
- ¼ teaspoon salt
- 1/8 teaspoon pepper
- 1 tablespoon Balsamic vinegar

Directions:

1. Add a cup of water to Ninja Foodi, place steamer basket, and add tilapia in the basket. Season with pepper and salt.
2. Close Ninja Foodi, press the steam button and Set the temperature time to 2 min.
3. Mix black pepper, olive oil, salt, basil, garlic, and tomatoes, then mix well.
4. Once done cooking, do a quick release.
5. Serve and enjoy with the basil-tomato dressing.

Nutrition Values Per Serving:
Calories: 196, Carbohydrates: 2.0g, Protein: 20.0g, Total fats 12.0g

Tangy Catfish

Prep Time: 10 min Cooking Time: 13 min Servings: 2
Ingredients:

- 2 tbsp flour
- 1 teaspoon red chili powder
- ½ teaspoon paprika
- ½ teaspoon garlic powder
- Salt, as required
- 2 (6-ounces) catfish fillets
- 1 tablespoon olive oil

Directions:

1. Arrange the greased Air Fryer Basket into the Ninja Foodi's pot of Ninja Foodi.
2. Close the Ninja Foodi with a crisping lid and select "Air Crisp" mode.
3. Set the temperature 400 °F/ 204 °C for almost 5 min.
4. Press "Start/Stop" to begin preheating.
5. In a suitable bowl, mix the flour, paprika, garlic powder and salt.
6. Add the catfish fillets and coat with the mixture evenly.
7. Now, coat each fillet with oil.
8. After preheating, open the lid.
9. Place the catfish fillets into the Air Fryer Basket.
10. Close the Ninja Foodi with a crisping lid and select "Air Crisp" mode.
11. Set the temperature 400 °F/ 204 °C for almost 13 min.
12. Hit the "Start/Stop" button to initiate cooking.
13. Flip the fish fillets once cooked halfway through.
14. Open the lid and serve hot.

Nutrition Values Per Serving:
Calories: 458, Total fat: 34.2g, Fiber: 3.7g, Carbohydrates: 7.5, Protein: 32g

Parmesan Crusted Tilapia

Prep Time: 10 min Cooking Time: 4 hours Servings: 4
Ingredients:
- 45 g Parmesan cheese, sliced in grater
- 57 g mayonnaise
- 59 ml fresh lemon juice
- Salt and black pepper, as required
- 4 (4-ounce) tilapia fillets
- 2 tbsp fresh cilantro, chopped

Directions:
1. In a suitable bowl, mix all ingredients except tilapia fillets and cilantro.
2. Coat the fillets with a mayonnaise mixture evenly.
3. Place the filets over a large piece of foil.
4. Wrap the foil around fillets to seal them.
5. Arrange the foil packet at the bottom of Ninja Foodi.
6. Close the Ninja Foodi with a crisping lid and select "Slow Cook".
7. Set on "Low" and cook for 3-4 hours.
8. Hit the "Start/Stop" button to initiate cooking.
9. Remove the lid and transfer the foil parcel onto a platter.
10. Open the parcel and serve hot with the garnishing of cilantro.

Nutrition Values Per Serving:
Calories: 190, Total fat: 8.5g, Fiber: 2g, Carbohydrates: 3.9g, Protein: 25g

Sea Bass Curry

Prep Time: 2 min Cooking Time: 3 min Servings: 2
Ingredients:
- 1 can coconut milk
- Juice, 1 lime
- 1 tablespoon red curry paste
- 1 teaspoon fish sauce
- 1 teaspoon coconut aminos
- 1 teaspoon honey
- 2 teaspoon sriracha
- 2 cloves garlic, minced
- 1 teaspoon ground turmeric
- 1 teaspoon ground ginger
- ½ teaspoon of sea salt
- ½ teaspoon white pepper
- 1-pound sea bass, cut into 1" cubes
- 4 g chopped fresh cilantro
- 2 lime wedges

Directions:
1. Mix black pepper, ginger, salt, garlic, sriracha, turmeric, honey, red curry paste, coconut aminos, fish sauce, lime juice, and coconut milk in a suitable bowl.
2. Place fish in the pot and pour coconut milk mixture over it.
3. Close the Ninja Foodi, press the pressure button, at high, and cook for 3 min.
4. Once done cooking, do a quick release.
5. Serve and enjoy with equal amounts of lime wedge and cilantro.

Fish Coconut Curry

Prep Time: 5 min Cooking Time: 15 min Servings: 2
Ingredients:

- 1-lb fish steaks or fillets, rinsed and cut into bite-size pieces
- 1 tomato, chopped
- 1 green chile, julienned
- 1 small onion, julienned
- 2 garlic cloves, squeezed
- ½ tbsp sliced in grater ginger
- 2 bay laurel leaves
- 1 teaspoon ground coriander
- 1 teaspoon ground cumin
- ½ teaspoon ground turmeric
- ½ teaspoon Chilli powder
- ½ teaspoon ground fenugreek
- 250 ml unsweetened coconut milk
- Salt to taste

Directions:

1. Press the sauté button and heat the oil.
2. Add garlic, sauté for a minute. Stir in ginger and onions.
3. Sauté for 5 min. Stir in bay leaves, fenugreek, Chilli powder, turmeric, cumin, and coriander.
4. Sauté for 1 minute, then pour in coconut milk to deglaze the pot.
5. Stir in tomatoes and green chilies. Mix well.
6. Add fish and mix well.
7. Cover the pressure lid. Press the pressure cook button, select low settings and cook for 5 min.
8. Once done cooking, do a quick release.
9. Serve and enjoy.

Nutrition Values Per Serving:
Calories: 434, Carbohydrates: 11.7g, Protein: 29.7g, Total fats 29.8g

Mixed Seafood Stew

Prep Time: 5 min Cooking Time: 35 min Servings: 2
Ingredients:

- 1 tablespoon vegetable oil
- ½ 14.5-oz can fire-roasted tomatoes
- 52 g diced onion
- 45 g chopped carrots
- 118 ml of water
- 120 mL white wine or broth
- 1 bay leaf
- ½ tablespoon tomato paste
- 1 tablespoon minced garlic
- 1 teaspoon fennel seeds toasted and ground

- ½ teaspoon dried oregano
- 1 teaspoon salt
- 1 teaspoon red pepper flakes
- 224 g mixed seafood
- 1 tablespoon fresh lemon juice

Directions:
1. Press sauté button on Ninja Foodi and heat oil.
2. Once hot, stir in onion and garlic. Sauté for 5 min.
3. Stir in tomatoes, bay leaves, tomato paste, oregano, salt, and pepper flakes. Cook for 5 min.
4. Stir in bell pepper, water, wine, and fennel seeds. Mix well.
5. Close Ninja Foodi, press the pressure button, select high settings, and Set the temperature time to 15 min.
6. Once done cooking, do a quick release.
7. Stir in defrosted mixed seafood.
8. Cover and let it cook for 10 min in the residual heat.
9. Serve and enjoy with a dash of lemon juice.

Nutrition Values Per Serving:
Calories: 202, Carbohydrates: 10.0g, Protein: 18.0g, Total fats 10.0g

Salmon with Orange Sauce

Prep Time: 3 min Cooking Time: 15 min Servings: 2
Ingredients:

- 1-pound salmon
- 1 tablespoon dark soy sauce
- 2 teaspoon minced ginger
- 1 teaspoon minced garlic
- 1 teaspoon salt
- 1 ½ teaspoon ground pepper
- 2 tbsp low sugar marmalade

Directions:
1. In a heatproof pan that fits inside your Ninja Foodi, add salmon.
2. Mix all the sauce ingredients and pour over the salmon. Allow marinating for 15-30 min. Cover pan with foil securely.
3. Put 473 ml of water in Ninja Foodi and add the trivet.
4. Place the pan of salmon on the trivet.
5. Cover the pressure lid. Press the pressure cook button, select Low settings, and cook for 5 min.
6. Once done cooking, do a quick release.
7. Serve and enjoy.

Nutrition Values Per Serving:
Calories: 177, Carbohydrates: 8.8g, Protein: 24.0g, Total fats 5.0g

Herbed Cod Parcel

Prep Time: 15 min Cooking Time: 8 min Servings: 2
Ingredients:

- 2 (4-ounce) cod fillets
- ½ teaspoon garlic powder
- Salt and black pepper, as required

- 2 fresh dill sprigs
- 4 lemon slices
- 2 tbsp butter

Directions:

1. Place 1 fillet in the center of one parchment square.
2. Drizzle garlic powder, salt and black pepper over each fillet.
3. Top each of these fillets with 2 lemon slices, 1 dill sprig, and 1 tablespoon butter.
4. Fold each parchment paper around the fillets to seal.
5. Into the Ninja Foodi's pot of Ninja Foodi, place 1 cup of water.
6. Arrange the "Reversible Rack" into the Ninja Foodi's pot of Ninja Foodi.
7. Place the fish parcels over the "Reversible Rack".
8. Close the Ninja Foodi pressure lid and place the pressure valve to the "Seal" position.
9. Select "Pressure" and set it to "High for 8 min.
10. Hit the "Start/Stop" button to initiate cooking.
11. Once done, release the pressure naturally then remove the lid.
12. Open the lid and transfer the fish parcels onto serving plates.
13. Carefully unwrap the parcels and serve.

Nutrition Values Per Serving:
Calories: 227, Total fat: 12.9g, Fiber: 3g, Carbohydrates: 10.3g, Protein: 22g

Salmon with Dill Sauce

Prep Time: 10 min Cooking Time: 2 hours Servings: 6
Ingredients:

- 470 ml water
- 96 g chicken broth
- 2 tbsp fresh lemon juice
- 2.5 g fresh dill, chopped
- ½ teaspoon lemon zest, sliced in grater
- 6 (4-ounce) salmon fillets
- Salt and black pepper, as required

Directions:

1. Into the Ninja Foodi's pot of Ninja Foodi, mix the water, broth, lemon juice, lemon juice, dill and lemon zest.
2. Arrange the prepared salmon fillets on top, skin side down and sprinkle with salt and black pepper.
3. Close the Ninja Foodi with a crisping lid and select "Slow Cook" mode. Set on "Low" for 1-2 hours.
4. Hit the "Start/Stop" button to initiate cooking.
5. Open the lid and serve hot.

Nutrition Values Per Serving:
Calories: 164, Total fat: 7.7g, Fiber: 1g, Carbohydrates: 1.6g, Protein: 23g

Spinach Scallops

Prep Time: 15 min Cooking Time: 15 min Servings: 3
Ingredients:

- 1 (10-ounce) package spinach, drained

- 12 sea scallops
- Olive oil cooking spray
- Salt and black pepper, as required
- 180 g heavy whipping cream
- 1 tablespoon tomato paste
- 1 teaspoon garlic, minced
- 1 tablespoon fresh basil, chopped

Directions:
1. Arrange the greased Air Fryer Basket into the Ninja Foodi's pot of Ninja Foodi.
2. Close the Ninja Foodi with a crisping lid and select "Air Crisp" mode.
3. Set the temperature 350 °F/ 177 °C for almost 5 min.
4. In the bottom of a 7-inch heatproof pan, place the spinach.
5. Spray each scallop with cooking spray and then sprinkle with a little salt and black pepper.
6. Arrange scallops on top of the spinach in a single layer.
7. In a suitable bowl, add the cream, tomato paste, garlic, basil, salt and black pepper and mix well.
8. Place the cream mixture over the spinach and scallops evenly.
9. After preheating, open the lid.
10. Place the pan into Air Fryer Basket.
11. Close the Ninja Foodi with a crisping lid and select "Air Crisp" mode.
12. Set the temperature 350 °F/ 177 °C for almost 10 min.
13. Hit the "Start/Stop" button to initiate cooking.
14. Open the lid and serve hot.

Nutrition Values Per Serving:
Calories: 234, Total fat: 12.4g, Fiber: 2.3g, Carbohydrates: 8.4g, Protein: 23g

---

Sweet Mahi-Mahi

Prep Time: 4 min Cooking Time: 10 min Servings: 2
Ingredients:
- 2 6-oz mahi-mahi fillets
- Salt
- Black pepper, to taste
- 1-2 cloves garlic, minced or crushed
- 1" piece ginger, finely sliced in grater
- ½ lime, juiced
- 2 tbsp honey
- 1 tablespoon nana mi togarashi
- 2 tbsp sriracha
- 1 tablespoon orange juice

Directions:
1. In a heatproof dish that fits inside the Ninja Foodi, mix well orange juice, sriracha, Nanami togarashi, honey-lime juice, ginger, and garlic.
2. Season mahi-mahi with pepper and salt.
3. Place in a bowl of sauce and cover well in the sauce. Seal dish securely with foil.
4. Add a cup of water in Ninja Foodi, place trivet, and add a dish of mahi-mahi on a trivet.
5. Close Ninja Foodi, press the steam button and Set the temperature time to 10 min.
6. Once done cooking, do a quick release.

7.   Serve and enjoy.
Nutrition Values Per Serving:
Calories: 200, Carbohydrates: 20.1g, Protein: 28.1g, Total fats 0.8g

---

Salmon Pasta

Prep Time: 5 min Cooking Time: 10 min Servings: 2
Ingredients:

- 4 ounces dry pasta
- 237 ml of water
- 3-ounces smoked salmon, broken in bite-sized pieces
- ¼ lemon
- Salt and black pepper
- ½ teaspoon sliced in grater lemon zest
- ½ teaspoon lemon juice
- 2 tbsp heavy cream
- 1 tablespoon walnuts
- 1 clove garlic
- 30 g packed baby spinach
- 1 ½ tbsp olive oil
- 22 g sliced in grater parmesan + more for serving/garnish
- Kosher Salt and black pepper, to taste
- 1 teaspoon sliced in grater lemon zest
- 60 g heavy cream

Directions:
1.   Make the sauce in a blender by pulsing garlic and walnuts until chopped.
2.   Add ¼ teaspoon pepper, ¼ teaspoon salt, ½ cup parmesan, oil, and 2/3 of spinach. Puree until smooth.
3.   Add butter, water, and pasta in Ninja Foodi.
4.   Cover and seal the pressure lid.
5.   Close Ninja Foodi, press the pressure button, select high settings, and Set the temperature time to 4 min.
6.   Once done cooking, do a quick release.
7.   Press stop and then press sauté.
8.   Stir in remaining parmesan, remaining spinach, sauce, lemon juice, lemon zest, heavy cream, and smoked salmon. Mix well and sauté for 5 min.
9.   Serve and enjoy.
Nutrition Values Per Serving:
Calories: 465, Carbohydrates: 31.0g, Protein: 20.1g, Total fats 29.0g

Chapter 6-Vegetarian Recipes

Buttered Green Peas

Prep Time: 10 min Cooking time: 17 min Servings: 5
Ingredients:

- 260 g green peas
- 30 g fresh mint
- 1 tablespoon dried mint
- 237 ml of water
- 1 teaspoon salt
- 1 tablespoon butter
- ½ teaspoon peppercorn
- 1 teaspoon olive oil

Directions:
1. Wash the mint and chop it. Transfer the chopped mint to the Ninja Foodi.
2. Add water and close the Ninja Foodi's lid.
3. Cook the mixture on the "Pressure" mode for 7 min.
4. Strain the mint leaves from the water and discard them.
5. Add green peas, dried mint, salt, peppercorn to the liquid into the Ninja Foodi's pot, and Close the Ninja's lid.
6. Cook the dish in the "Pressure" mode for 10 min.
7. Rinse the cooked green peas in a colander.
8. Put the peas in the serving bowl and add butter and olive oil.
9. Stir the cooked dish gently until the butter is dissolved.

Nutrition Values Per Serving:
Calories: 97, Total fat: 4.6g, Fiber: 4g, Carbohydrates: 11.48g, Protein: 3g

Turmeric Turnip Fries

Prep Time: 15 min Cooking time: 14 min Servings: 5
Ingredients:

- 1-pound turnips, peeled
- 1 tablespoon avocado oil
- 1 teaspoon dried oregano
- 1 teaspoon onion powder
- ½ teaspoon salt
- 1 teaspoon turmeric

Directions:
1. Cut the turnips into the fries and sprinkle them with the dried oregano, avocado oil, onion powder, and turmeric.
2. Mix the turnip and let it soak the spices for 5-10 min.
3. After this, place them in the Ninja basket and Close the Ninja's lid.
4. Set "Air Crisp" cooking mode at 390F and cook the fries for 14 min.
5. Stir the turnips fries twice during the cooking.
6. When the meal gets a light brown color, it is cooked.

7. Transfer it to the serving plates and sprinkle it with salt.
Nutrition Values Per Serving:
Calories: 34, Total fat: 0.4g, Fiber: 1.9g, Carbohydrates: 7g, Protein: 0.9g

Sweet Tomato Salsa

Prep Time: 10 min Cooking time: 8 min Servings: 6
Ingredients:
- 400 g tomatoes, chopped
- 1 teaspoon sugar
- 5 g fresh cilantro
- 2 white onions, chopped
- 1 teaspoon black pepper
- 1 teaspoon cayenne pepper
- ½ jalapeno pepper, chopped
- 1 teaspoon olive oil
- 1 tablespoon minced garlic
- 60 g of green olives
- 1 teaspoon paprika
- 7 g basil
- 1 tablespoon Sugar

Directions:
1. Transfer the vegetables to the Ninja Foodi and sprinkle them with olive oil.
2. Close the Ninja's lid and cook the ingredients on the" Steam" mode for 8 min.
3. Meanwhile, wash the tomatoes and chop them.
4. Place the chopped tomatoes in the bowl. Chop the cilantro.
5. Add the chopped cilantro, black pepper, Chilli pepper, and minced garlic in the chopped tomatoes.
6. Add green olives, chop them or leave them whole as desired.
7. Chop the basil and add it to the salsa mixture. Add paprika and olive oil.
8. Once cooked, transfer the veggies from the Ninja Foodi to a plate.
9. Chop the vegetables and add them to the salsa mixture. Sprinkle the dish with Sugar.
10. Mix well and serve.

Nutrition Values Per Serving:
Calories: 41, Total fat: 1.1g, Fiber: 1.9g, Carbohydrates: 7.7g, Protein: 1.2g

Cheesy Dumplings

Prep Time: 10 min Cooking time: 15 min Servings: 6
Ingredients:
- 225 g cottage cheese
- 68 g flour
- 1 teaspoon baking soda
- 1 teaspoon salt
- 2 tbsp Sugar
- 4 tbsp coconut milk
- 1 teaspoon basil
- 3 eggs

Directions:
1. Blend the cottage cheese in a blender, add eggs and continue blending until smooth.

2. Transfer the mixture to the bowl and add baking soda and flour.
3. Top the mixture with salt, sugar, coconut milk, and basil. Knead the dough.
4. Make the small logs from the dough.
5. Set the temperature Ninja Foodi mode to "Steam," transfer the dough logs to the Ninja Foodi, and Close the Ninja's lid.
6. Cook for 15 min. Once it is done, remove the dumplings from the Ninja Foodi.
7. Serve immediately.

Nutrition Values Per Serving:
Calories: 102, Total fat: 6.5g, Fiber: 0.5g, Carbohydrates: 2.6g, Protein: 8.7g

Creamy Asparagus Mash

Prep Time: 6 min Cooking time: 6 min Servings: 1
Ingredients:

- 87 g asparagus
- 118 ml of water
- 1 tablespoon heavy cream
- 1 tablespoon fresh basil, chopped
- ½ teaspoon salt
- ¾ teaspoon lemon juice

Directions:
1. Put asparagus in the Ninja cooker. Add water and salt.
2. Close and seal the lid. Cook the vegetables on "Pressure" cooking mode for 6 min.
3. Open the lid and drain half of the liquid. Add fresh basil.
4. Using the hand blender, blend the mixture until smooth.
5. Then add lemon juice and heavy cream. Stir the mash and transfer it into the serving bowls.

Nutrition Values Per Serving:
Calories: 67, Total fat: 5.7g, Fiber: 1.5g, Carbohydrates: 3.2g, Protein: 1.9g

Eggplant Turnip Casserole

Prep Time: 10 min Cooking time: 20 min Servings: 8
Ingredients:

- 3 eggplants, chopped
- 1 white onion, chopped
- 1 bell pepper, chopped
- 1 turnip, chopped
- 1 teaspoon salt
- 1 teaspoon black pepper
- 1 teaspoon cayenne pepper
- ½ teaspoon white pepper
- 231 g cream
- 5 oz Parmesan, sliced in grater

Directions:
1. Mix white onion, bell pepper, and turnip.
2. Add salt, black pepper, cayenne pepper, and white pepper.
3. In the cooker place, eggplants. Then add the layers of onion mixture.
4. Add cheese and cream. Close and seal the lid.
5. Cook the casserole for 10 min on" Pressure" cooking mode.

6.   Then make quick pressure release, then serve warm.
Nutrition Values Per Serving:
Calories: 144, Total fat: 6g, Fiber: 8.1g, Carbohydrates: 17.3g, Protein: 8.5g

Turmeric Cauliflower Rice

Prep Time: 10 min Cooking time: 5 min Servings: 2
Ingredients:
- 107 g cauliflower
- 1 tablespoon turmeric
- ½ teaspoon onion powder
- ½ teaspoon garlic powder
- 1 teaspoon dried dill
- ½ teaspoon salt
- 1 teaspoon butter
- 2 pecans, chopped
- 118 ml of water

Directions:
1.   Chop the cauliflower roughly and place it in the food processor.
2.   Pulse it 3-4 time or until you get cauliflower rice.
3.   After this, transfer the vegetables to the cooker.
4.   Add onion powder, garlic powder, dried dill, and salt.
5.   Then add chopped pecans and water.
6.   Stir the mixture gently with the help of the spoon and Close the Ninja's lid.
7.   Cook it on" Pressure" cooking mode for 5 min.
8.   Then use quick pressure release and open the lid.
9.   Drain the water using the colander.
10. Transfer the cauliflower rice to the big bowl, add turmeric and butter.
11. Mix the mixture well. Serve it warm.
Nutrition Values Per Serving:
Calories: 145, Total fat: 12.3g, Fiber: 3.6g, Carbohydrates: 8.1g, Protein: 3.1g

Spicy Green Beans

Prep Time: 10 min Cooking time: 15 min Servings: 8
Ingredients:
- 12 ounces green beans
- 1 teaspoon garlic powder
- 1 teaspoon onion powder
- 4 garlic cloves
- 2 tbsp olive oil
- 1 teaspoon cayenne pepper
- 1 jalapeno pepper
- 1 teaspoon butter
- ½ teaspoon salt
- 237 ml of water

Directions:

1. Wash the green beans and cut each into two equal parts.
2. Toss the green beans in a suitable mixing bowl.
3. Sprinkle the vegetables with onion powder, Chilli pepper, and salt and stir.
4. Remove all the seeds from the jalapeno and chop finely.
5. Add the chopped jalapeno1 to the green bean's mixture.
6. Peel the garlic and slice it. Mix the sliced garlic with olive oil.
7. Blend the mixture and transfer it to the Ninja Foodi.
8. Add the water and stir. Put the green beans in the Ninja Foodi and Close the Ninja's lid.
9. Set the temperature Ninja Foodi mode to" Sauté," and cook the vegetables for 15 min.
10. Once cooked, you should have firm but not crunchy green beans.
11. Remove the green beans from the Ninja Foodi and discard the liquid before serving.

Nutrition Values Per Serving:
Calories: 49, Total fat: 4.1g, Fiber: 1g, Carbohydrates: 3g, Protein: 1g

Green Pepper Tomato Salsa

Prep Time: 7 min Cooking time: 10 min Servings: 5
Ingredients:

- 200 g tomatoes
- 1 teaspoon cumin
- 1 teaspoon ground coriander
- 1 tablespoon cilantro
- 15 g fresh parsley
- 1 lime
- 1 sweet green pepper
- 1 red onion
- 1 teaspoon garlic powder
- 1 teaspoon olive oil
- 5 garlic cloves

Directions:
1. Remove the seeds from the sweet green pepper and cut it in half.
2. Peel the onion and garlic cloves. Place the vegetables in the Ninja Foodi and sprinkle them with ½ teaspoon of olive oil.
3. Close the Ninja's lid, and Set the temperature Ninja Foodi to" Sauté" mode for 10 min.
4. Meanwhile, chop the tomatoes and parsley.
5. Peel the lime and squeeze the juice from it.
6. Mix the lime juice with the chopped parsley, cilantro, ground coriander, and garlic powder and stir well.
7. Sprinkle the chopped tomatoes with the lime mixture.
8. Remove the vegetables from the Ninja Foodi.
9. Rough chop the bell pepper and onions and add the ingredients to the tomato mixture.
10. Mix well and serve.

Nutrition Values Per Serving:
Calories: 38, Total fat: 1.2g, Fiber: 1g, Carbohydrates: 6.86g, Protein: 1g

Bok Choy with Mustard Sauce

Prep Time: 10 min Cooking time: 12 min Servings: 7

Ingredients:
- 1-pound bok choy
- 237 ml of water
- 85 ml of soy sauce
- 1 teaspoon salt
- 1 teaspoon red Chilli flakes
- 5 tablespoon mustard
- 80 g cream
- 1 teaspoon cumin seeds
- 1 teaspoon black pepper
- 1 tablespoon butter
- 34 g garlic clove

Directions:
1. Wash the bok choy and chop it into pieces.
2. Mix water, soy sauce, salt, Chilli flakes, cumin seeds, and black pepper together.
3. Blend the mixture. Peel the garlic clove and cut into thin slices.
4. Add the butter in the Ninja Foodi and sliced garlic.
5. Set the temperature Ninja Foodi to" Sauté" mode and sauté for 1 minute.
6. Add the cream, soy sauce mixture, and bok choy. Close the Ninja's lid.
7. Set the temperature pot to "Sauté" mode and cook for 10 min.
8. Drain the water from the Ninja Foodi and sprinkle the bok choy with the mustard, stirring well.
9. Cook for 2 min on the manual mode, then transfer the dish to the serving plate.
10. Enjoy.

Nutrition Values Per Serving:
Calories: 83, Total fat: 4.8g, Fiber: 2.1g, Carbohydrates: 7.4g, Protein: 4.2g

Parmesan Tomatoes

Prep Time: 7 min Cooking time: 7 min Servings: 5
Ingredients:
- 10 ounces big tomatoes
- 7 ounces Parmesan cheese
- ½ teaspoon paprika
- 3 tbsp olive oil
- 1 tablespoon basil
- 1 teaspoon cilantro
- 1 teaspoon onion powder

Directions:
1. Wash the tomatoes and slice them into thick slices.
2. Spray the Ninja Foodi with olive oil inside.
3. Transfer the tomato slices to the Ninja Foodi.
4. Mix the paprika, basil, and cilantro and mix well.
5. Grate the Parmesan cheese and sprinkle the tomato slices with the cheese and spice mixture.
6. Close the Ninja Foodi's lid and cook on the" Sauté" mode for 7 min.
7. Once it is done, open the Ninja Foodi's lid and let the tomatoes rest briefly.
8. Transfer the dish to the serving plate.

Nutrition Values Per Serving:
Calories: 250, Total fat: 19.3g, Fiber: 1g, Carbohydrates: 7.85g, Protein: 12g

Cheesy Zucchini

Prep Time: 10 min Cooking time: 10 min Servings: 6
Ingredients:

- 1-pound yellow zucchini
- 3 tbsp minced garlic
- 56 g coconut flour
- 3 tbsp olive oil
- 3 eggs
- 57 g of coconut milk
- 7 ounces Romano cheese
- 1 teaspoon salt

Directions:
1. Wash the zucchini and slice them. Mix the minced garlic and salt and stir the mixture.
2. Mix the minced garlic mixture and zucchini slices and mix well.
3. Add the eggs to the suitable mixing bowl and whisk the mixture.
4. Add coconut milk and coconut flour. Stir it carefully until combined.
5. Grate the Romano cheese and add it to the egg mixture and mix.
6. Pour the olive oil in the Ninja Foodi and preheat it.
7. Dip the sliced zucchini into the egg mixture.
8. Transfer the dipped zucchini to the Ninja Foodi and cook the dish in the" Sauté" mode for 2 min on each side.
9. Once cooked, remove it from the Ninja Foodi, drain any excess fat using a paper towel, and serve.

Nutrition Values Per Serving:
Calories: 301, Total fat: 21.6g, Fiber: 5.1g, Carbohydrates: 12.5g, Protein: 16g

Seasoned Deviled Eggs

Prep Time: 15 min Cooking time: 5 min Servings: 7
Ingredients:

- 1 tablespoon mustard
- 60 g cream
- 1 teaspoon salt
- 8 eggs
- 1 teaspoon mayonnaise
- 2.25 g dill
- 1 teaspoon ground white pepper
- 1 teaspoon minced garlic

Directions:
1. Put the eggs in the Ninja Foodi and add water.
2. Cook the eggs at high pressure for 5 min.
3. Remove the eggs from the Ninja Foodi and chill.
4. Peel the eggs and cut them in half. Remove the egg yolks and mash them.
5. Add the mustard, cream, salt, mayonnaise, ground white pepper, and minced garlic to the mashed egg yolks.
6. Chop the dill and sprinkle the egg yolk mixture with the dill. Mix well until smooth.
7. Transfer this egg yolk mixture to a pastry bag fill the egg whites with the yolk mixture.
8. Serve immediately.

Nutrition Values Per Serving:
Calories: 170, Total fat: 12.8g, Fiber: 0g, Carbohydrates: 2.42g, Protein: 11g

Vegetable Salad with Cheese

Prep Time: 10 min Cooking time: 15 min Servings: 7
Ingredients:
- 2 medium carrots
- 7 ounces turnips
- 1 tablespoon olive oil
- 1 red onion
- 4 garlic cloves
- 5 ounces feta cheese
- 1 teaspoon butter
- 1 teaspoon onion powder
- 1 tablespoon salt
- 1 teaspoon black pepper
- 1 red sweet bell pepper

Directions:
1. Put all the vegetables in the Ninja Foodi and cook them in the "Steam" mode for 15 min.
2. Chop the cooked vegetables into small pieces.
3. Mix them in a suitable mixing bowl. Add butter and stir.
4. Top the mixture with onion powder, salt, black pepper.
5. Add feta cheese and add rest of the components to the salad.
6. Mix well and serve.

Nutrition Values Per Serving:
Calories: 107, Total fat: 6.9g, Fiber: 1.6g, Carbohydrates: 8.2g, Protein: 3.8g

Black Peas Pickled Garlic

Prep Time: 10 min
Cooking time: 9 min
Servings: 12
Ingredients:

- 270 g garlic
- 1 tablespoon salt
- 1 tablespoon olive oil
- 1 teaspoon fennel seeds
- ½ teaspoon black peas
- 709 mL of water
- 5 tablespoon apple cider vinegar
- 1 teaspoon lemon juice
- 1 teaspoon lemon zest
- 1 tablespoon stevia
- 1 teaspoon red Chilli flakes

Directions:

1. Place the salt, olive oil. Fennel seeds, black peas, lemon juice, lemon zest, stevia, and Chilli flakes in the Ninja Foodi.
2. Add water and stir it. Preheat the liquid on the" Pressure" mode for 5 min.
3. Meanwhile, peel the garlic. Put the garlic into the preheated liquid.
4. Add apple cider vinegar and stir the mixture.
5. Close the Ninja's lid and cook the garlic on the" Pressure" mode for 4 min.
6. Open the Ninja Foodi's lid and leave the garlic in the liquid for 7 min.
7. Transfer the garlic to the liquid into a glass jar, such as a Mason jar.
8. Seal the jar tightly and keep it in your refrigerator for at least 1 day before serving.

Nutrition Values Per Serving:
Calories: 46, Total fat: 1.3g, Fiber: 0.6g, Carbohydrates: 7.7g, Protein: 1.5g

---

Herbed Radish

Prep Time: 10 min Cooking time: 8 min Servings: 5

Ingredients:

- 340 g radish, trimmed
- 1 tablespoon olive oil
- 1 tablespoon butter
- 1 teaspoon salt
- 1 teaspoon dried dill

Directions:

1. Cut the radishes into halves and place them into the mixing bowl.
2. Sprinkle them with olive oil, salt, and dried dill.
3. Give a good shake to the vegetables.
4. After this, transfer them to the Ninja cooker and add butter.
5. Close the Ninja's lid and set "Air Crisp" cooking mode.
6. Cook the radishes for 8 min at 375°F/190°C.
7. Stir the radish once cooked half way through.
8. Transfer the radishes to the serving plates and serve them hot.

Nutrition Values Per Serving:
Calories: 56, Total fat: 5.2g, Fiber: 1.1g, Carbohydrates: 2.5g, Protein: 0.5g

---

Soft Cloud Bread

Prep Time: 15 min Cooking time: 7 min Servings: 4

Ingredients:

- 1 egg
- ¾ teaspoon cream of tartar
- 1 tablespoon cream cheese
- ¾ teaspoon onion powder
- ¾ teaspoon dried cilantro

Directions:

1. Separate egg white from egg yolk and place them into the separated bowls.
2. Whisk the egg white with the cream of tartar until the strong peaks.
3. After this, whisk the cream cheese with the egg white until fluffy.
4. Add onion powder and dried cilantro. Stir gently.
5. After this, carefully add egg white and stir it.

6. Scoop the mixture into the Ninja cooker to get small "clouds" and lower the crisp lid.
7. Cook the bread for 7 min at 360°F/ °C/183°C or until it is light brown.
8. Allow it to cool then serve.

Nutrition Values Per Serving:
Calories: 27, Total fat: 0.2g, Fiber: 0g, Carbohydrates: 0.9g, Protein: 1.6g

Butternut Squash Fries

Prep Time: 10 min Cooking time: 15 min Servings: 5
Ingredients:
- 1-pound butternut squash
- 1 teaspoon salt
- 59 ml of water
- 2 tbsp turmeric
- 3 tbsp peanut oil

Directions:
1. Wash the butternut squash and peel it. Cut the butternut squash into strips.
2. Sprinkle the cubes with salt, turmeric, and peanut oil.
3. Stir the mixture well. Place the butternut squash strips into the Ninja Foodi and set it to" Sauté" mode.
4. Sauté the vegetables for 10 min. Stir the mixture frequently.
5. Add water and close the Ninja Foodi's lid.
6. Cook the dish on" Pressure" mode for 5 min.
7. Once it is done, the butternut squash cubes should be tender but not mushy.
8. Transfer the dish to the serving plate and rest briefly before serving.

Nutrition Values Per Serving:
Calories: 124, Total fat: 8.3g, Fiber: 3g, Carbohydrates: 13.13g, Protein: 1g

Zucchini Noodles

Prep Time: 10 min Cooking time: 10 min Servings: 6
Ingredients:
- 2 medium green zucchinis
- 1 tablespoon wine vinegar
- 1 teaspoon white pepper
- ½ teaspoon cilantro
- ¼ teaspoon nutmeg
- 200 ml chicken stock
- 1 garlic clove

Directions:
1. Wash the zucchini and use a spiralizer to make the zucchini noodles.
2. Peel the garlic and chop it.
3. Mix the cilantro, chopped garlic clove, nutmeg, and white pepper in a suitable mixing bowl.
4. Sprinkle the zucchini noodles with the spice mixture.
5. Pour the chicken stock in the Ninja Foodi and sauté the liquid on the manual mode.
6. Add the zucchini noodles and wine vinegar and stir the mixture gently.
7. Cook for 3 min on the" Sauté" mode.
8. Remove the zucchini noodles from the Ninja Foodi and serve.

Nutrition Values Per Serving:

Calories: 28, Total fat: 0.7g, Fiber: 1g, Carbohydrates: 3.94g, Protein: 2g

---

Marinated Olives

Prep Time: 10 min Cooking time: 17 min Servings: 7
Ingredients:
- 540 g olives
- 1 tablespoon red Chilli flakes
- 1 teaspoon cilantro
- 79 ml olive oil
- 4 tbsp apple cider vinegar
- 3 tbsp minced garlic
- 79 ml of water
- 3 garlic cloves
- 1-ounce bay leaf
- 60 ml of water
- 1 teaspoon clove
- 4 tbsp lime juice

Directions:
1. Mix the Chilli flakes, cilantro, apple cider vinegar, minced garlic, bay leaf, water, and lime juice in a suitable mixing bowl.
2. Add the chopped garlic to the Chilli flake mixture and sprinkle it with the garlic.
3. Add water and place the mixture in the Ninja Foodi.
4. Close the Ninja's lid and cook it in the" Pressure" mode for 10 min.
5. Once it is done, remove the mixture from the Ninja Foodi and transfer it to a sealed container.
6. Add olive oil and olives then cook on Sauté mode for 7 min.
7. Serve.

Nutrition Values Per Serving:
Calories: 186, Total fat: 16.9g, Fiber: 4g, Carbohydrates: 10.57g, Protein: 1g

---

Parsley Carrot Fries

Prep Time: 10 min Cooking time: 18 min Servings: 2
Ingredients:
- 2 carrots, peeled
- 1 teaspoon salt
- 1 tablespoon olive oil
- 1 teaspoon dried parsley

Directions:
1. Cut the carrots into the fries and sprinkle with the salt and dried parsley.
2. Mix well and transfer them into the ninja cooker.
3. Close the Ninja's lid and cook the fries on the "Air Crisp" mode for 18 min at 385 °F/ °C.
4. Once done, remove the Ninja's lid and toss well.
5. Serve.

Nutrition Values Per Serving:
Calories: 85, Total fat: 7g, Fiber: 1.5g, Carbohydrates: 6g, Protein: 0.5g

Chapter 7-Desserts Recipes

Soft Cinnamon Bun

Prep Time: 10 min Cooking time: 15 min Servings: 8
Ingredients:

- 136 g   flour
- ½ teaspoon baking powder
- 3 tablespoon Sugar
- 2 tablespoon ground cinnamon
- ½ teaspoon vanilla extract
- 1 tablespoon butter
- 1 egg, whisked
- ¾ teaspoon salt
- 85 g almond milk

Directions:
1. Mix the flour, baking powder, vanilla extract, egg, salt, and almond milk.
2. Knead the soft and non-sticky dough.
3. Roll the prepared dough using a rolling pin on a floured surface.
4. Sprinkle dough with butter, cinnamon, and Sugar.
5. Roll the dough into the log and cut the roll into 7 pieces.
6. Spray Ninja Foodi Air Fryer's insert with the cooking spray.
7. Place the cinnamon buns in the basket and Close the Ninja's lid.
8. Cook on the "Bake/Roast" cooking mode and cook the buns for 15 min at 355 °F/ 179 °C.
9. Allow the buns to cool and serve.

Nutrition Values Per Serving:
Calories: 127, Total fat: 10.5g, Fiber: 3g, Carbohydrates: 22g, Protein: 4g

Pumpkin Cupcakes

Prep Time: 7 min Cooking time: 20 min Servings: 5
Ingredients:

- 1 tablespoon butter, melted
- 1 tablespoon pumpkin puree
- 1 teaspoon ground cinnamon
- ¼ teaspoon ground ginger
- 1 egg, beaten
- 3 tablespoon Sugar
- 68 g flour
- ½ teaspoon baking powder

Directions:
1. Mix butter, cinnamon and all of the ingredients in a suitable mixing bowl.
2. Transfer the mixture into the silicone muffin molds and place in the Ninja Foodi.
3. Cover the Ninja Foodi's lid and Cook on the "Bake/Roast" cooking mode.
4. Cook the muffins for 20 min at 330 °F/ 166 °C.
5. Serve.

Nutrition Values Per Serving:
Calories: 52, Total fat: 4.6g, Fiber: 0.7g, Carbohydrates: 23g, Protein: 1.8g

Pecan Muffins

Prep Time: 10 min Cooking time: 12 min Servings: 6
Ingredients:

- 4 tablespoon butter, softened
- 4 tablespoon coconut flour
- 1 egg, whisked
- 4 tablespoon heavy cream
- ½ teaspoon vanilla extract
- 1 tablespoon pecans, crushed
- 2 tablespoon sugar

Directions:

1. Mix coconut flour, butter, egg, heavy cream, vanilla extract, and sugar in a suitable mixing bowl.
2. Use the hand mixer to mix the mixture until smooth.
3. Pour the smooth batter into the silicone muffin molds.
4. Top every muffin with the pecans and transfer in Ninja Foodi rack.
5. Cover the Ninja Foodi's lid and Cook on the "Bake/Roast" cooking mode.
6. Cook the pecan muffins for 12 min at 350 °F/ °C.
7. Serve!

Nutrition Values Per Serving:
Calories: 170, Total fat: 15.1g, Fiber: 3.6g, Carbohydrates: 31.1g, Protein: 2.8g

Creamy Pumpkin Pie

Prep Time: 10 min Cooking time: 25 min Servings: 6
Ingredients:

- 1 tablespoon pumpkin puree
- 112 g coconut flour
- ½ teaspoon baking powder
- 1 teaspoon apple cider vinegar
- 1 teaspoon Pumpkin spices
- 1 tablespoon butter
- 60 g heavy cream
- 2 tablespoon liquid stevia
- 1 egg, whisked

Directions:

1. Mix with the apple cider vinegar, melted butter, heavy cream, stevia, egg, and baking powder in a suitable mixing bowl.
2. Add pumpkin puree, coconut flour, pumpkin spices and stir the batter until smooth.
3. Pour the batter in the Ninja Foodi basket and cover the Ninja Foodi's lid.
4. Set the temperature "Bake/Roast" cooking mode at 360°F /183°C.
5. Cook the pie for 25 min.
6. Let the pie chill till room temperature
7. Serve it.

Nutrition Values Per Serving:
Calories: 127, Total fat: 6.6g, Fiber: 8.1g, Carbohydrates: 28g, Protein: 3.8g

Zesty Cake

Prep Time: 8 min Cooking time: 62 min Servings: 6
Ingredients:

- 1 teaspoon dried mint
- 112 g coconut flour
- 1 teaspoon baking powder
- 50 g Sugar
- 2 eggs, whisked
- 60 g heavy cream
- 1 tablespoon butter
- ½ teaspoon lemon zest, sliced in grater

Directions:
1. In a suitable mixing bowl, mix all the ingredients.
2. Use the cooking machine to make the soft batter from the mixture.
3. Pour the batter into the Ninja Foodie basket and flatten it well.
4. Close the Ninja Foodi's lid and set "Pressure" cooking mode. Seal the lid.
5. Cook the cake on Low pressure for 55 min.
6. Then cover the Ninja Foodi's lid and set "Air Crisp" cooking mode.
7. Cook the cake for 7 min more at 400 °F/ 204 °C.
8. Chill the cake well and serve!

Nutrition Values Per Serving:
Calories: 136, Total fat: 7.2g, Fiber: 8.1g, Carbohydrates: 22g, Protein: 4.7g

Easy Vanilla Custard

Prep Time: 5 min Cooking time: 15 min Servings: 4
Ingredients:

- 3 egg yolks
- 240 mL almond milk
- 1 teaspoon vanilla extract
- 2 tablespoon sugar

Directions:
1. Whisk egg yolk and Sugar.
2. Add vanilla extract and almond milk.
3. Preheat your Ninja Foodi cooker at Sauté/Sear cooking mode at 365 °F/185°C for 5 min
4. Then pour the almond milk mixture and sauté it for 10 min.
5. Stir the liquid all the time.
6. Transfer it into the serving jars and leave it for 1 hour in the fridge.
7. Serve it!

Nutrition Values Per Serving:
Calories: 181, Total fat: 17.7g, Fiber: 1.3g, Carbohydrates: 32g, Protein: 3.4g

Chocolaty Lava Cakes

Prep Time: 6 min Cooking time: 8 min Servings: 2
Ingredients:

- 2 eggs, whisked

- 3 tbsp flax meal
- 2 teaspoon of cocoa powder
- ½ teaspoon baking powder
- 2 tbsp heavy cream
- Cooking spray

Directions:
1. Spray the cake cups with the cooking spray inside.
2. Mix all the remaining ingredients and pour the mixture into the prepared cups.
3. Cover the cups with foil and place them in Ninja Foodi.
4. Cook on the "Bake/Roast" cooking mode 355 °F/ 179 °C.
5. Close the Ninja's lid and cook the dessert for 8 min.
6. Serve the cooked lava cups hot!

Nutrition Values Per Serving:
Calories: 165, Total fat: 13.9g, Fiber: 3.6g, Carbohydrates: 5.3g, Protein: 8.4g

Cinnamon Vanilla Bites

Prep Time: 10 min Cooking time: 12 min Servings: 5
Ingredients:

- 1 teaspoon ground cinnamon
- 150 g flour
- ½ teaspoon baking powder
- 1 teaspoon olive oil
- 85 g almond milk
- 1 teaspoon butter
- ½ teaspoon vanilla extract
- 237 ml water for cooking

Directions:
1. Mix all the dry ingredients.
2. Then add butter and almond milk to the dry ingredients.
3. Add vanilla extract and olive oil and knead the smooth and non-sticky dough.
4. Make the medium sized balls from the prepared dough and place them in the silicone molds.
5. Pour water in Ninja Foodi Air Fryer's insert.
6. Place the molds on the rack in Ninja Foodi.
7. Close the Ninja's lid and seal it.
8. Set "Pressure" cooking mode at High.
9. Cook the cinnamon bites for 10 min on the set mode.
10. Once done, naturally release the pressure for 10 min.
11. Then remove the liquid from the basket and cover the Ninja Foodi's lid.
12. Set Air Crisp and cook the bites for 2 min more.
13. Serve!

Nutrition Values Per Serving:
Calories: 180, Total fat: 15.2g, Fiber: 2.9g, Carbohydrates: 19g, Protein: 5.1g

Vanilla Coconut Muffins

Prep Time: 7 min Cooking time: 2 min Servings: 4
Ingredients:
- 4 tablespoon coconut flour

- 1 teaspoon coconut shred
- 1 teaspoon vanilla extract
- 1 egg, beaten
- 1 tablespoon sugar
- ¼ teaspoon baking powder
- 237 ml water for cooking

Directions:
1. Whisk coconut flour with all the ingredients in a suitable until lump-free.
2. Add water in the Ninja Foodi Air Fryer insert.
3. Place the batter into the muffin molds and transfer them on the Ninja Foodi rack.
4. Cover the Ninja Foodi's lid and set "Pressure" cooking mode at High.
5. Cook the muffins for 2 min. Use the quick pressure release method.
6. Let the muffins cool and serve!

Nutrition Values Per Serving:
Calories: 61, Total fat: 2.9g, Fiber: 3.3g, Carbohydrates: 27g, Protein: 2.5g

Chocolate Brownies

Prep Time: 10 min Cooking time: 5 min Servings: 5
Ingredients:
- 45 g flour
- 1 tablespoon sugar
- 60 g heavy cream
- ½ teaspoon vanilla extract
- 3 tbsp cocoa powder
- 3 tbsp butter
- 1 oz dark chocolate

Directions:
1. Place the flour in the springform pan and flatten to make the layer.
2. Then place the springform pan into the Ninja Foodi's pot and cover the Ninja Foodi's lid.
3. Cook the flour for 3 min at 400 °F/ 204 °C or until the flour gets a golden color.
4. Meanwhile, mix cocoa powder and heavy cream.
5. Add vanilla extract and Sugar.
6. Remove the flour from Ninja Foodi and chill well.
7. Toss butter and dark chocolate into the Ninja Foodi's pot and cook for 1 minute on Sauté/Sear cooking mode.
8. Stir in the heavy cream mixture.
9. Then add chocolate and flour, mix until smooth.
10. Serve.

Nutrition Values Per Serving:
Calories: 159, Total fat: 14.9g, Fiber: 2.1g, Carbohydrates: 21g, Protein: 2.5g

Raspberry Cake

Prep Time: 10 min Cooking time: 30 min Servings: 10
Ingredients:
- 168 g coconut flour
- 1 teaspoon baking powder

- 1 teaspoon lemon juice
- 62.5 g raspberries
- 50 g sugar
- 1 egg, whisked
- 79 ml almond milk
- 1 tablespoon butter, melted
- ½ teaspoon vanilla extract

Directions:
1. Mix all the dry ingredients.
2. Then add egg, almond milk, and butter.
3. Add vanilla extract and lemon juice.
4. Stir the mixture well. You have to get a liquid batter.
5. Place the layer of the raspberries in the silicone mold.
6. Pour batter over the raspberries.
7. Place the mold on the rack and insert it into the Ninja Foodi basket.
8. Close the Ninja Foodi's lid and Cook on the "Bake/Roast" cooking mode.
9. Cook the cake for 30 min at 350 °F/ 177 °C.
10. Turn the cake upside down on a plate and transfer it to the serving plate.
11. Enjoy!

Nutrition Values Per Serving:
Calories: 107, Total fat: 4.5g, Fiber: 8.9g, Carbohydrates: 25.1g, Protein: 4.3g

Savory Donuts

Prep Time: 20 min Cooking time: 10 min Servings: 5
Ingredients:
- 204 g flour
- ½ teaspoon baking soda
- 1 teaspoon vanilla extract
- 1 egg, whisked
- 2 tbsp sugar
- 120 g heavy cream

Directions:
1. Mix the whisked egg, heavy cream, sugar, vanilla extract, and baking soda.
2. When the mixture is homogenous, add flour.
3. Stir well and knead the non-sticky dough.
4. Let the dough rest for 10 min.
5. After this, roll the dough with the help of the rolling pin into 1 inch thick.
6. Then make the donuts with the help of the cutter.
7. Select the Ninja Foodi "Bake/Roast" cooking mode and set 360°F/183°C.
8. Place the donuts in the basket and cover the Ninja Foodi's lid.
9. Cook the donuts for 5 min.
10. Chill the donuts well and serve!

Nutrition Values Per Serving:
Calories: 118, Total fat: 11.5g, Fiber: 1g, Carbohydrates: 24g, Protein: 2.7g

Mini Chocolate Cakes

Prep Time: 10 min Cooking time: 22 min Servings: 3
Ingredients:

- 1 tablespoon cocoa powder
- 4 tbsp flour
- ½ teaspoon vanilla extract
- 1 tablespoon sugar
- 80 g heavy cream
- ¼ teaspoon baking powder
- Cooking spray

Directions:
1. Mix the flour, cocoa powder, heavy cream, sugar, vanilla extract, and baking powder.
2. Use the mixer to make the smooth batter.
3. Spray the silicone molds with the cooking spray inside.
4. Pour the batter into the silicone molds and transfer then in Ninja Foodi Air Fryer's insert.
5. Close the Ninja Foodi's lid and set Bake-Roast Option.
6. Cook the cakes at 255 °F/124 °C for 22 min.
7. Serve the dessert chilled!

Nutrition Values Per Serving:
Calories: 108, Total fat: 9.6g, Fiber: 1.6g, Carbohydrates: 32g, Protein: 2.6g

Vanilla Brownie

Prep Time: 10 min Cooking time: 32 min Servings: 6
Ingredients:
- 3 tbsp sugar
- 1 oz chocolate chips
- 2 eggs, whisked
- ½ teaspoon vanilla extract
- 3 tablespoon butter, melted
- 1 tablespoon flour

Directions:
1. Whisk the melted butter, flour, vanilla extract, and Sugar.
2. Melt the chocolate chips and add them to the butter mixture.
3. Add eggs and stir until smooth.
4. Pour the batter into Ninja Foodi Air Fryer's insert, select "Bake/Roast" cooking mode and cook at 360°F/183°C for 32 min.
5. Then check if the brownie cooked and chill well.
6. Cut it into the servings and serve!

Nutrition Values Per Serving:
Calories: 99, Total fat: 8.8g, Fiber: 0.1g, Carbohydrates: 19g, Protein: 2.4g

Gingered Cookies

Prep Time: 10 min Cooking time: 14 min Servings: 7
Ingredients:

- 150 g flour
- 3 tbsp butter
- 1 egg
- ½ teaspoon baking powder
- 3 tablespoon sugar
- 1 teaspoon ground ginger
- ½ teaspoon ground cinnamon
- 3 tbsp heavy cream

Directions:

1. Beat the egg in suitable bowl and whisk it gently.
2. Add baking powder, sugar, ground ginger, ground cinnamon, heavy cream, and flour.
3. Stir gently and add butter, then Knead the non-sticky dough.
4. Roll the prepared dough with the help of the rolling pin and make the cookies with the help of the cutter.
5. Place the cookies in the basket in one layer and Close the Ninja's lid.
6. Cook on the "Bake/Roast" cooking mode and cook the cookies for 14 min at 350 °F/ 177 °C.
7. Serve.

Nutrition Values Per Serving:
Calories: 172, Total fat: 15.6g, Fiber: 1.8g, Carbohydrates: 31g, Protein: 4.4g

Cocoa Avocado Mousse

Prep Time: 10 min Cooking time: 2 min Servings: 7
Ingredients:

- 2 avocados, peeled, cored
- 1 teaspoon of cocoa powder
- 80 g heavy cream
- 1 teaspoon butter
- 3 tbsp sugar
- 1 teaspoon vanilla extract

Directions:

1. Preheat your Ninja Foodi cooker at "Sauté/Sear" cooking mode for 5 min.
2. Meanwhile, mash the avocado until smooth and mix it with sugar.
3. Place the butter into the Ninja Foodi's pot and melt.
4. Add mashed avocado mixture and stir well.
5. Add cocoa powder and stir until homogenous. Sauté the mixture for 3 min.
6. Meanwhile, whisk the heavy cream at high speed for 2 min.
7. Transfer the cooked avocado mash to the bowl and chill in ice water.
8. Add whisked heavy cream and vanilla extract. Stir gently to get swirls.
9. Transfer the mousse into small cups and chill for 4 hours in the fridge.
10. Serve!

Nutrition Values Per Serving:
Calories: 144, Total fat: 13.9g, Fiber: 3.9g, Carbohydrates: 15g, Protein: 1.3g

Sweet Almond Bites

Prep Time: 10 min Cooking time: 14 min Servings: 5
Ingredients:

- 1 egg, whisked
- 150 g flour
- ¼ cup almond milk
- 1 tablespoon coconut flakes
- ½ teaspoon vanilla extract
- ½ teaspoon baking powder
- ½ teaspoon apple cider vinegar
- 2 tbsp butter

Directions:

1. Mix the whisked egg, almond milk, baking powder, apple cider vinegar, vanilla extract, and butter.
2. Stir the mixture and add flour and coconut flakes. Knead the dough.
3. Make the medium balls from the dough and place them on the rack of Ninja Foodi.
4. Press them gently with the hand palm.
5. Cover the Ninja Foodi's lid and cook the dessert for 12 min at 360°F/ 183°C.
6. Enjoy!

Nutrition Values Per Serving:
Calories: 118, Total fat: 11.5g, Fiber: 1g, Carbohydrates: 2.4g, Protein: 2.7g

Chocolate Chip Cookies

Prep Time: 10 min Cooking time: 9 min Servings: 8
Ingredients:

- 1 oz chocolate chips
- 3 tablespoon butter
- 150 g flour
- 1 egg, whisked
- 2 tbsp sugar

Directions:

1. Mix the flour and whisked the egg.
2. Add butter and sugar, and mix the mixture until homogenous.
3. Add chocolate chips and knead the homogenous dough.
4. Make 8 small balls from the dough and transfer them to the rack of Ninja Foodi.
5. Close the Ninja Foodi's lid and Cook on the "Bake/Roast" cooking mode.
6. Cook the chip cookies for 9 min at 360°F/183°C.
7. Chill the cookies and serve!

Nutrition Values Per Serving:
Calories: 145, Total fat: 12.3g, Fiber: 1.5g, Carbohydrates: 12g, Protein: 3.9g

Blackberry Vanilla Cake

Prep Time: 8 min Cooking time: 20 min Servings: 4
Ingredients:

- 4 tbsp butter
- 3 tablespoon sugar
- 2 eggs, whisked
- ½ teaspoon vanilla extract
- 1 oz blackberries
- 150 g flour
- ½ teaspoon baking powder

Directions:

1. Mix all the liquid cake ingredients.
2. Then add baking powder, flour, and Sugar.
3. Stir the mixture until smooth.
4. Add blackberries and stir the batter gently with the help of the spoon.
5. Take the non-sticky springform pan and transfer the batter inside.
6. Place the springform pan into the Ninja Foodi's pot and cover the Ninja Foodi's lid.
7. Cook the cake for 20 min at 365 °F/ 185 °C.
8. Chill it and serve!

Nutrition Values Per Serving:
Calories: 173, Total fat: 16.7g, Fiber: 1.1g, Carbohydrates: 32g, Protein: 4.2g

Zucchini Crisps

Prep Time: 5 min Cooking time: 10 min Servings: 4
Ingredients:

- 1 zucchini, chopped

- 1 teaspoon Vanilla extract
- 2 tablespoon sugar
- 1 tablespoon coconut flakes
- 2 tablespoon butter
- 1 tablespoon flour

Directions:
1. Preheat your Ninja Foodi cooker at Sauté/Sear cooking mode for 5 min at 360°F/183°C.
2. Toss the butter in the Ninja Foodi Air Fryer insert.
3. Add chopped zucchini and Sauté the vegetables for 3 min.
4. Add vanilla extract, coconut flakes, Sugar, and stir well.
5. Cook the zucchini for 4 min more.
6. Then add flour and stir well.
7. Sauté the dessert for 1 minute.
8. Cook on the "Air Crisp" cooking mode for 2 min to get a crunchy crust.
9. Serve the cooked dessert immediately!

Nutrition Values Per Serving:
Calories: 84, Total fat: 8.5g, Fiber: 0.5g, Carbohydrates: 26g, Protein: 0.3g

Creamy Coconut Pie

Prep Time: 6 min Cooking time: 10 min Servings: 4
Ingredients:
- 1 tablespoon coconut flour
- 5 oz coconut, shredded
- ½ teaspoon vanilla extract
- 1 tablespoon sugar
- 1 teaspoon butter
- 1 egg, whisked
- 60 g heavy cream

Directions:
1. Mix the coconut flour, coconut shred, and butter.
2. Stir the mixture until homogenous.
3. Add the whisked egg, vanilla extract, Sugar, and heavy cream. Stir well.
4. Transfer the pie mixture into the basket and cover the Ninja Foodi's lid.
5. Cook on the "Bake/Roast" cooking mode 355 °F/ 179 °C.
6. Cook the pie for 10 min.
7. Check if the pie is cooked with the help of the toothpick and chill it tills the room temperature
8. Serve it!

Nutrition Values Per Serving:
Calories: 185, Total fat: 16.9g, Fiber: 3.9g, Carbohydrates: 22g, Protein: 3g

Cashew Butter Cookies

Prep Time: 10 min Cooking time: 11 min Servings: 7
Ingredients:
- 1 tablespoon sugar
- 1 egg, whisked
- 6 oz cashew butter

Directions:

1. Mix all the ingredients and make the small balls.
2. Place the balls in the basket of Ninja Foodi and Close the Ninja's lid.
3. Cook on the "Bake/Roast" cooking mode and cook the cookies at 330°F/165°C for 11 min.
4. Serve!

Nutrition Values Per Serving:
Calories: 152, Total fat: 12.6g, Fiber: 0.5g, Carbohydrates: 18g, Protein: 5.1g

Mini Vanilla Cheesecakes

Prep Time: 30 min Cooking time: 4 min Servings: 4
Ingredients:

- 8 tbsp cream cheese
- 4 tablespoon sugar
- 2 tbsp heavy cream
- ½ teaspoon vanilla extract
- 4 tbsp flour

Directions:
1. Whisk the cream cheese and heavy cream in a suitable mixing bowl.
2. Add vanilla extract and stir again.
3. Scoop the medium balls from the cream cheese mixture.
4. Mix the flour and all the remaining Sugar.
5. Then coat every cheesecake ball into the flour mixture.
6. Freeze the prepared balls for 20 min or until they are solid.
7. Place the cheesecake balls in the Ninja Foodi basket and cover the Ninja Foodi's lid.
8. Cook the dessert at 400 °F/ 204 °C for 4 min.
9. Enjoy.

Nutrition Values Per Serving:
Calories: 139, Total fat: 13.1g, Fiber: 0.8g, Carbohydrates: 23g, Protein: 3.2g

Creme Brulee

Prep Time: 20 min Cooking time: 10 min Servings: 3
Ingredients:

- 231 g heavy cream
- 4 egg yolks
- 3 tbsp sugar
- ½ teaspoon vanilla extract

Directions:
1. Beat egg yolks with 2 tbsp sugar in a suitable bowl.
2. Add heavy cream and stir until homogenous.
3. Place the mixture into the ramekins and cover them with the foil.
4. Make the small holes on the top of the foil with the help of the toothpick.
5. Pour ½ cup of water into Ninja Foodi basket and insert trivet.
6. Place the ramekins on the trivet and close the Ninja Foodi's lid.
7. Cook the dessert on "Pressure" cooking mode at High for 10 min.
8. Then make the quick pressure release for 5 min.
9. Let the dessert chill for 10 min.
10. Remove the foil from the ramekins and sprinkle the creme Brulee with Sugar.
11. Use the hand torch to caramelize the surface.
12. Serve it!

Nutrition Values Per Serving:

Calories: 212, Total fat: 20.8g, Fiber: 0g, Carbohydrates: 37g, Protein: 4.4g

Pumpkin Pudding

Prep Time: 10 min Cooking time: 25 min Servings: 4

Ingredients:

- 3 eggs, whisked
- ½ teaspoon vanilla extract
- 4 tbsp pumpkin puree
- 1 teaspoon pumpkin pie spices
- 231 g heavy cream
- 2 tablespoon sugar
- 237 ml water for cooking

Directions:

1. Whisk the eggs, pumpkin puree, vanilla extract, pumpkin pie spices, cream, and Sugar.
2. Pour the liquid into the non-stick cake pan.
3. Pour water into the Ninja Foodi's pot.
4. Place the pudding in a cake pan into the Ninja Foodi's pot on the rack and Close the Ninja's lid.
5. Select Steam mode and cook the dessert for 25 min.
6. Let the cooked pudding rest for 10 min then open the lid.
7. Place it in the fridge for a minimum of 4 hours.
8. Enjoy!

Nutrition Values Per Serving:

Calories: 159, Total fat: 14.5g, Fiber: 0.5g, Carbohydrates: 27g, Protein: 5g

Thank you for Reaching at the end of the book

Hope you enjoyed your time with this book

Scan and follow the instructions to get your Gift

Printed in Great Britain
by Amazon

61572430R00061